What are people saying about *The Ultimate Power* . . .

"Wow—what a great book. If you are ready to turn on your Ultimate Power, read Ken's brilliant and illuminating book."

—Mark Victor Hansen, Co-author of
Chicken Soup for the Soul
New York Times #1 Bestseller

"Reading like a fast-paced novel, the book invites—no urges—the reader to choose life. To use the gifts of the heart and mind to their fullest."

—Dr. Jonathan Siegel, Psychologist

"The book was music to my ears, mind and soul. I felt the power of Ken's journey. Read the book and your life will be richer for it."

—Hennie Bekker, Canadian Juno Award Nominee

"After meeting Ken for an article focusing on his remarkable life story, I was inspired by his energy, vision and determination. In his book, The Ultimate Power, *Ken recounts many of life's unexpected turns, giving readers insight into how one can rebound from a shattered life to come out on top."*

—Rob Andrus, Freelance Journalist

"Without a scintilla of doubt, Ken's book delivers the goods."

—Barry Seltzer, TV show host/personality, Lawyer, Co-author of
It Takes 2 Judges to Try a Cow and Other Strange Legal Twists

"Quite honestly, I'm not the type of person who buys "self-help" books. That being the case, I approached your manuscript with a degree of caution—okay skepticism—and was then rewarded with a great read. This is definitely a compliment to you and your story-telling ability. Your story is compelling and I think most readers will find it so."

—Phyllis Schwager, Freelance Editor

"The Ultimate Power will be an inspiration to anyone who reads it. It is the story of turning challenges into opportunities to grow, and it is filled with a sense of humor to make it digestible."

—Cavett Robert, Chairman Emeritus,
National Speakers Association

"Extraordinary experiences, extraordinary life. Compelling reading, important insights for those seeking to better their lives."

—Pamela Sims, M.Ed., Education, Consultant and Author

"Instantly I felt The Ultimate Power's *authenticity. Listen to its message—when you're ready, you will hear the message—and rediscover your personal power."*

—Jacqueline Brant

"As I was reading the book, I began to feel myself transforming, growing into a better person. Wow!"

—Daniel Jones

"No one can truly understand a problem until they have experienced it. The Ultimate Power *describes one man's struggle to recover from a catastrophic injury. It is a compelling story which lights the way for others and shows that healing is indeed possible for us all."*

—Dr. Michael Greenwood, M.B., B. Chir., Dip. Acup, C.C.F.P., F.R.S.A.
Co-author *Paradox and Healing*

What are people saying about Ken's stories and inspiring motivational speeches?

"As one professional speaker to another, your keynote presentation was incredibly inspirational, entertaining and unforgettable!"
—Paul Waller, Seminar Manager, Canadian Plastics Institute

"Your visual imagery is vivid and powerfully delivered. Move over Dylan Thomas—now we have A Child's Christmas in Willowdale."
—Bruce Tempest, Toastmaster

"Your ideas inspired my students and me all year. Thanks."
—Benjamin Shefler, Professor, Seneca College

"Thank you for coming and delivering a very inspiring presentation on self-motivation. I could see my students enjoying it!"
—Bernie Silverman, Central Commerce Collegiate

"Your message and wit were super! Your enthusiasm contagious!"
—Dale Smith

"You manage to capture the subtleties in our lives that we often overlook and it is these things that bring the greatest of pleasure."
—Mary Savona

Dear Reader, Meeting Planner and Speakers Bureau:

Make your convention or meeting a memorable experience. Book Ken Vegotsky as your keynote speaker, or seminar/workshop facilitator. Ken is an entertaining educator. As an added bonus Ken shares the stage with his persona—Gramps: Down Home Wisdom from a City Slicker™. A good time is guaranteed for all!

Ken says, "May I always give you more than you pay for. May you always want to pay me more." That is Ken's philosophy and a fact!

Please contact:

Masterpiece Corporation Speakers and Trainers Bureau™
One Babington Court
Islington, Ontario Canada M9A 1J7
Tel (416) 239-6300
Fax (416) 232-9343

MEMBER
NATIONAL
SPEAKERS
ASSOCIATION

The Ultimate Power

How To Unlock Your Mind-Body-Soul Potential

The Ultimate Power

How To Unlock Your Mind-Body-Soul Potential

by

Ken Vegotsky

AGES Publications
Los Angeles, California, U.S. & Toronto, Ontario, Canada

THE LOVE LIVING & LIVE LOVING SERIES™

Manufactured in the United States of America   First printing 1995
                    10 9 8 7 6 5 4 3 2 1
Library of Congress Cataloging-in-Publication Data
Vegotsky, Ken, 1951-
    The ultimate power : how to unlock your
mind-body-soul potential / by Ken Vegotsky
    p. cm. — (The love living & live loving series)
    Includes bibliographical references and index.
    ISBN 1-886508-15-1 (pbk) -- ISBN 1-886508-17-8 (audio-tape)
    1. New thought. 2. Vegotsky, Ken, 1951- 3. Mind and body.
    4. Self-actualization (Psychology) 5. Mental healing --Case studies.
I. Title.   II. Series.
BF639.V44 1994
158? . 1--dc20   94-24030

National Library of Canada Cataloging-in-Print Data
Vegotsky, Ken, 1951-
    The ultimate power : lessons from a near death
experience : how to unlock your mind-body-soul potential

(The love living & live loving series ; 1)
Includes bibliographical references and index.

ISBN 1-896280-18-8 Volume 1
1. Self-help techniques.   2. Self-actualization
(Psychology). I. Title. II. Series.

BF632.V44 1995   155.2   C94-932358-6

Cover Design: Falcom Design & About Books, Inc.
ATTENTION ORGANIZATIONS, COLLEGES, UNIVERSITIES AND CORPORATIONS: This book is available at special quantity discounts for bulk purchases for premiums, sales promotions, fund-raising, special books, booklets, or excerpts can also be created to meet your specific needs. For information write Special Markets Department, Adi, Gaia, Esalen Publications, Inc., 8391 Beverly Blvd., Suite 323-S, Los Angeles, California 90048 or call 1-800-652-8574

Dedication

I dedicate this book to you, the reader.
You are making a difference, each and every day.

Mission Statement

I vow each and every day, to share with you the miracles I have found in this greatest of gifts called life. My mission is not to change the world but fine-tune it for my children, all children.

—Ken Vegotsky

Acknowledgments

I acknowledge with thanks:

The medical professionals and others, too numerous to list, who helped me learn to help myself.

My editors and test readers Liba Berry, Phyllis Schwager, Lynne Shuttleworth, Lynn Teatro and Wendy Thomas—for their insights and professionalism.

Mark Field, Linda Pellowe, Fortunato Aglialoro, Tom and Marilyn Ross who guided me through the business of getting published—along with a host of others, too numerous to list.

The hundreds of authors and writers whose works I read over the last twelve years, during my struggle to survive and thrive, in a world gone awry.

The staff at Micro Boutique, Apple Power Macintosh 6100/60AV, ClarisWorks software and Peter Miller, the computer whiz—who made it so much easier.

Preface

No longer can I stand by and watch life pass me by. My struggles helped me realize life is a rare and beautiful gift. I cherish all these fine folks who help make mine a joy.

My children, Stephanie and Alan, who brighten my life immeasurably. Mom for being there. Mark Grossman for nurturing my desire to share my story. Laini, my ex-wife and mother of two wonderful children. Sheri, Alex, Carla, Louis, Joni, Rob, Amanda, Ryan, Jeff, Joanne, Ruth, Charlie, Linda, Barry, Glyn, Helen, Shael, Evelyn, Bessie, Donna, Gary, Sharon, Norman, Arlene, Denis, Molly, Paul, Stan, Honey, Glen, Natalie, Sam, Sheldon, Richard, Jeannie, Marla, Ed, Willie, Felix, Jonathan, Mike, Alissa, Roz, Brad, Bruce, Fran, Ken, Al, Maureen, Jimmy, Cy, David, Peter, Elaine, Chris, Bill, Arabella, Fraser and all those folks who were there before, during and after the events portrayed in this book.

My health care givers who showed me how to help myself.

Toastmasters International and the National Speakers Association, great people and self-help groups.

Finally, the most important person of all at this time—*you!* The reader. Your efforts to become a better person by buying this book are the greatest acknowledgement of support I can get. Together we will make this a better world. One person at a time.

May I always give you more than you pay for.
May you always want to pay me more.

—Ken Vegotsky

Table of Contents

Foreword

Seek and ye shall find. This is Ken's wake-up call of hope and promise to people in pain, those who suffer emotionally and anyone who wants a better life. In a homespun narrative with universal appeal, Ken Vegotsky recounts his personal descent into a living nightmare, a nightmare that began with a serious accident which left him paralyzed and in pain. Reading like a fast-paced novel, the book invites—no, urges—the reader to choose life. To use the gifts of the heart and mind to their fullest. Writing with sincerity and enthusiasm, Ken offers readers hope, a promise for spiritual awakening and a new relationship to living.

Every day, I work with patients who are in chronic pain. I see them struggle as they search for solutions to their suffering and a cure for their pain. Inevitably, these patients enter a negative cycle that begins with despair and self-loathing and leads eventually to blaming others for their suffering. The chronic pain sufferer ends up feeling alone, helpless, hopeless and dependent on others for happiness. Doctors, friends and family may reach out with various strategies for relief, but the pain invariably continues until that person undergoes a fundamental change in attitude.

Weaving his hard-earned insights with personal anecdotes, Ken Vegotsky helps sufferers move from victims to empowered human beings. By learning how to control his pain, Ken transformed his sense of self and opened a door to his very soul. While he did not eliminate his pain, the book clearly shows that the pain no longer controls him. Not surprisingly, Ken's formula for a healthier perspective on life emerges alongside his willingness to listen to his heart and resolve to take the initiative and use his mind in search of a higher power—what he calls a universal intelligence.

This book is divided into two parts. In the first part, he shares his personal experience and humanity, which allows the reader to bear witness to the path of his spiritual journey. In the second part of the book, Ken provides stories, insights, examples and exercises that encourage readers to find personal understanding and fulfillment. The exercises offer strong motivation for living—with or without pain.

As a psychologist—and a human being—I recommend this book to people who suffer chronic pain as well as to people who are searching for their authentic voice and a new beginning to life.

—Jonathan Siegel, Psychologist

Prologue

My Story

Nearly dying has a way of bringing you back to life.

It has been 12 years since I had my near-fatal parasailing accident—12 years of great pain, sorrow and tears, as well as laughter, growth and triumphs.

I am a 42-year-old partially paralyzed, divorced father of two kids. I have no job in the traditional sense, but I do have a desire to share with you the lessons I have learned in striving to survive and thrive again after my near-death experience. This is the story of the journey in which I discovered the mind-body-soul connection.

My personal transformation and the miracles of daily life that I became aware of evolved after my accident and during my recovery.

As you and I embark upon this journey of self-discovery, a renewed sense of awakening wells up inside me. I am honored to share with you the secrets of my successful recovery and inner growth. By sharing the keys to unlocking the mind-body-soul connection, I will achieve my mission in life and help you become fulfilled.

The greatest honor is to share with another person the miracle of believing and achieving. Thank you for sharing this journey with me.

Part I

Lessons from a Near-Death Experience

Chapter 1

Life's Journey

The jet's engines screeched as it came to a halt on the tarmac. Inside, the crowd of weary business travelers stood wrestling with their heavy winter coats while they waited to leave the plane. I felt the emotions of my first day at school—a mixture of fear and excitement.

Days before, I had been basking in the luxurious warmth of Los Angeles. That December, I had played tourist in the City of Angels for the first time during the four months I had been commuting there from Toronto. It was to be my last time in Los Angeles for a long time.

Laini, my lovely young wife, had flown out to the coast to join me and celebrate my thirtieth birthday. We had stayed at the Beverly Wilshire Hotel near Rodeo Drive, a minor earthquake being the only disturbance in an otherwise uneventful visit. Perhaps this was nature trying to warn me of what was to come.

I was facing a major personal business decision: move to Los Angeles, or leave Roadrunner Jeans Manufacturing Limited. I believed that a successful business operation demanded I relocate there. My partners did not share this belief, even though four years earlier I had transferred from Montreal to Toronto and successfully expanded our operation there.

By the age of 30, I had learned that the key to success is to live, breathe, and undertake all projects with an all-consuming passion. I had learned that what one was doing did not matter, as long as one was committed to it and persevered. Such is the wisdom of being on top of the world. On paper, I was worth a lot of money, but paper has

5

no value, I was soon to discover. People and their love, support and friendship are the true treasures in life.

I had been traveling from Toronto to Los Angeles once a week, while Laini stayed in Toronto. She was a real example of a woman of the '80s: running a home, working at a job and studying to become an accountant. She was a self-motivated, intelligent woman. This had its advantages. I could fly from city to city, work at a grueling pace and not be missed much at home.

The whirring sound of the plane's door opening signaled my arrival in Montreal. Suddenly, I was yanked from my dreams of Los Angeles, and unceremoniously pulled back to reality. A bone-chilling December wind rushed in to greet me, attacking the parts of my body not blanketed in my lambskin wool coat. Winter had arrived in the city with a vengeance the day before, I was told by a flight attendant. First the storm, then the aftermath of cleaning up.

I struggled with my carry-on bag and briefcase as I made my way through the terminal to a snow-covered world of idling cabs.

Entering the cab, I gave the driver the address in words as sharp and crisp as the morning air. I leaned back in the warm car and reminisced.

Four years earlier, I had moved to Toronto from Montreal. In that short time, I had developed the sales territory from thousands of dollars to $10 million in wholesale business. I had risen from the ranks of salaried sales rep to a partner in what was now a 50-million-dollar-plus clothing manufacturer and importer—at the time, the largest importer of moderately priced fashion goods from The People's Republic of China. Our success in business was to be our downfall.

I needed to clarify my future. The business travel was taking its toll on me and the business areas I was involved in. I believed that fate was what you made it, in business at least. I was in the manufacturing and import clothing business and my strength in sales was the key to my success. The customer always came first. It was simple, and for me it worked.

The cab pulled up to the front of the company head office. Roadrunner Jeans Mfg. Ltd. was emblazoned over the entrance. Lugging my bags, I left the taxi and made my way along the recently shoveled narrow path to the front door and into the reception area. After a brief hello to Susan, the receptionist, I put my bags in my office and proceeded down the hallway to the president's office to announce my arrival.

The president and 51 percent owner was sitting, phone in hand, feet propped up on his desk as he waved me in. I took a seat opposite him and waited. A few minutes later, he called in another partner. The president knew why I was there and as always was prepared. It was a lesson I had learned well at his side. Success is 90 percent preparation.

Greetings done, we got down to business. I told them I believed the business's future success depended on my moving to Los Angeles. I learned that if I did what I loved and was committed to it, the money followed. The president offered me back the sales position I had before taking on the Los Angeles assignment—without the power to make changes I felt necessary. This alternative was not acceptable to me. It did not take long. I immediately quit.

Months later, I found out about the problems the company was having. The president and vice president of finance shared very little information with me about the firm's financial condition. Since I was living out of town, there was a tendency on management's part to overlook my desire to be informed, even though I was a partner. However, it was just as much my fault as theirs. Traveling tends to distance one from the realities of daily business struggles. Money, new cars and perks kept coming so it had been easy for me to rationalize that things were okay.

I stayed overnight at my mom's, then made my way back home to Toronto the next day. During the following months, I used my successful sales past to acquire the rights to sell other clothing lines in the Toronto area. In the meantime, my lawyer played telephone and letter tag with my partners and their lawyer in an attempt to get money for my shareholdings in the business. Delegating this responsibility to my lawyer had a high price: time, energy and thousands of dollars.

I pursued other sales opportunities, successfully. Since February I had done my homework and by the end of June I'd obtained the rights to sell four clothing lines, planned my sales route and set up the business. The samples from the lines I was representing would not be available until mid-August. I had to wait until I had the samples before I could start selling.

Everything was in place, and at last I could take a break. Laini and I took the opportunity to go on vacation and chose to go to Nassau, Bahamas. Everything was looking great again. My life and future were at last back in my control.

7

Fate—The Accident

August 2, 1982

The parasailing dock was a short boat ride from our hotel. All day long, we watched as one person after another floated through the air, tethered to a brightly colored sail that was made into a parachute and pulled by a motorboat. The dreams of my childhood flew with each person in the sky. All morning long, the parasails seemed to beckon me, teasing my 30-year-old fantasy of flying. At long last, I knew I could and would.

Shortly after lunch, the motorboat came to get us. As it pulled up to the sand dune off the beach of our hotel, Laini and I got on board. A gentle breeze caressed my body as we sped off to the floating dock of tourists patiently waiting their turns to soar like eagles.

A group of 20 of us sat calmly on the dock that was attached to the sea floor a short distance from the beach. The gentle bobbing motion seemed to lull everyone into a state of relaxed anticipation. The tourists sat wearing their life jackets while three staff members on the dock controlled the comings and goings of the group.

It was Laini's turn. She stood up after the person before her landed. A large metal self-closing hook was placed through a metal ring attached to her life preserver. About 200 yards from the dock, the motorboat floated as Laini was given last-minute instructions. I listened intently to each word; my turn was next.

"Hold on to these handles. If you want to go to one side, gently tug on the handle on that side. I am going to signal the boat to rev its engine before it takes off. When my hand falls, start running slowly, the boat will do the rest of the work for you. Have a good flight," said Bob, the staff member. His tanned hand raised, then fell.

The boat's engine revved higher as the craft started to pick up speed, pulling the slack out of the water-soaked rope as it distanced itself from the dock. Suddenly, Laini was airborne. Only her legs were visible, dangling below the billowing parasail as she gracefully ascended skyward. My excitement increased with each moment. The seconds seemed like hours as the boat made a large circle pulling Laini behind it.

"You're next," Bob said as his hands checked the clasps on my orange life jacket. He lifted the large ring and gave it a gentle tug.

"How much do you weigh?" he asked.

"About 170 pounds," I answered.

He stared into my eyes, clearly doubting my answer, then grunted and said, "Sit down, I'll tell you when to get up. Wait until I call you." His message delivered as it had been thousands of times before, he turned his back on me and looked up at Laini as she was being pulled back toward us.

Moments later, the boat's engine quieted as it revved down and the craft began to drift forward. The idling sound from the engine was interrupted by the rope attached to Laini's life jacket as it clanged onto the dock and snapped through the metal tethering ring. The boat took up the slack from the rope as it drifted forward. Laini landed safely and, with a little help, unhooked herself from the life jacket. She looked completely exhilarated as she sat down.

Bob signaled me to stand and take her spot. Swiftly, the instructions he had given Laini were repeated for me. I nodded acknowledgment and suddenly found myself floating upward into the clear blue Nassau sky.

I could fly!

Peter Pan!

Eagles!

I was one with the birds as I felt the rushing wind on my face. The parachute sail flapped behind me as it caught the man-made breeze. Suddenly, a jolt hit me. The wind had filled my parasail and the rate of my ascent rapidly increased. I was taking my childhood flight. At long last.

The Dream Ends

August 5, 1982

I awoke for a moment. I felt my body bouncing in the confines of a metal fenced bed. I did not know where I was. Laini's eyes peered into my right eye. My left would not open. It did not concern me at the moment. It was all a dream. Moments earlier, I was soaring high in the sky, and now nothing seemed real . . . at first.

I knew I had died. I had been embraced by a great void in a place of total harmony—it was awesome. I mumbled a few words to that effect. Laini's head shook a no as she began to talk. The words did not make sense. I felt compelled to tell Laini what to do, in spite of battling a searing sensation in my eyes that distorted my vision. My mind and body sought and at last found refuge in the peacefulness of unconsciousness. I was in a drug-induced world, free from external signs of pain, in the minds of the hospital staff and Laini.

The First Message

August 6 & 7, 1982

I had touched the hand of death and found it wanting. I was not ready to die yet. The dreamlike images immediately after the accident beckoned to me, seducing me into an inner serenity. I had briefly visited a world of awesome tranquillity where I was at one with the universe.

Like a splash of ice water, the drugs drew me back to a distorted version of reality. The vision I was blanketed in became a jumble of pain, emotions and fear beyond anything I had ever experienced. Control had been wrested from me. I was at the mercy of those around me. They were trying their best, but all I wanted to do was scream out and cry for release.

"Please stop!" I yelled. No one heard. The overwhelming pain was winning. *"Please STOP!"* I begged. My mind and body were in agony. *"STOP! DAMN IT, STOP!"* The pain rolled on with ceaseless intensity. Like ocean waves as they reach their peak, slowly, persistently growing bigger and bigger. I was drowning in a sea of pain unaided by the very drugs meant to help me.

My screams could not be heard. They were inside me. At the time, I did not realize it was my mind that was yelling. My voice had been disconnected from my mind by the drugs and pain. It was there, but I could not use it.

It was many years before I understood that this pattern kept repeating itself. The love and kindness of others had become a test of my willpower. Like an opiate, the outside world promised to help, but the relief, if any, was temporary, and then the need was greater than before. In fact, the answers were within me. It was the gift of the message I received at that time that made it possible for me to go on. I knew I had a mission in life. Exactly what it was became obscured by the outside world's intervention. If the nurses, doctors, friends and family had allowed me to feel my pain, without intervention, the healing would have come sooner. At last I can say, "I forgive them, they knew not what they were doing."

The Gift

August 8, 1982

I awoke. My world was no longer focused within, as it had been moments before. My thoughts were jumbled.

Confusion and turmoil had taken over. I knew who I was a moment ago, but suddenly I had been thrust into the world of the living. Like a newborn child, I was reborn.

I started to turn my head to see the light beaming in from the window on my right.

"*OOOWWWEEE!*" I screamed in agony. I could not turn my head. Fear flooded my consciousness.

"*WHAT THE FUCK IS HAPPENING!*" I yelled. Across from me I could see blurs of white floating in my direction. The nurses had heard my cries.

Something was blocking the vision in my left eye. I reached up with my right hand to try to remove it, but before I could reach it, a hand gently grasped my arm. A blurry face covered my field of vision and said, "My name is Beth. I am your nurse. The doctor will be in shortly." She gently squeezed my arm.

"What's happening? Where am I?"

"You're in the Nassau General Hospital," she said in a thick island accent. "The doctor will answer your questions as soon as he gets here. Your wife is also here. They have gone to get her. Now take these pills and you will feel better."

"Water?" I asked as I reached for the offered pills. My throat was dry. I put the pills in my mouth and waited for the water. I tried to put the pills in my left hand so I could hold the water glass in my right hand. My left hand wasn't where I wanted it to be. Where was it? I wondered as another wave of pain hit me.

"Here's your water," Beth said, passing me a cup with a long straw in it. "Put the pills in your mouth and take a sip of water, s-l-o-w-l-y." Beth bent the straw toward my mouth.

"*OOOWWWEEE!*" I yelled. A searing pain stabbed at my left side. My body withered in agony. I gulped the pills and sucked the water, hoping to quicken my escape from the hellish pain. A look of satisfaction covered Beth's face as she turned and left, her job done.

It seemed like an eternity, yet it was only moments.

The pills had taken effect. I twisted my head toward the door, looking and praying for a familiar face to grace it. Where is Laini? I thought as another jolt of pain seized me. "God, please help me," I begged. My cries went unanswered as more pain consumed me. "Please," I pleaded, "please help." Tears obscured my vision, mingling with self-pity as I suffered and waited.

Laini's face suddenly appeared floating in an outburst of my tears. "My glaaassseeesss!" I said as the agony rolled on ceaselessly. For a moment, I had lost control of my speech. The simplest movement triggered the pain's ever-increasing intensity. My mind was numbed.

Anger! Fear! A mixed blessing in disguise that kept drawing me back to the here and now. It was a long while before I had relaxed enough to talk coherently with Laini. By then, the doctor had arrived.

"Mr. Vegotsky, I am Dr. Kassees. How are you?" he asked.

"I'm . . . " My voice trailed off as I was seized by another spasm of pain. Dr. Kassees waited patiently for me to regain control. Between the outbursts of agony and semicoherent speech, I was able to paint a picture of who I was and some of what had happened to me. Laini filled in the rest.

A shudder passed through her body as she recounted the details. My descent from the parasailing flight was too fast. The parasail and I were tethered to the boat. The boat had stopped and was idling in the water. Bob had signaled the boat to start moving again. By then, the rope had been put through the tether ring attached to the floating dock. My body crashed into the dock, bounced and ended up in the water. When they fished out my lifeless body, I was not breathing. First they resuscitated me, then rushed me to the hospital.

My memory of these events was blocked. The drugs given me and the journey I had taken during my "death" created too much chaos for my mind to sort out.

Whose fault the accident was did not matter. I knew that it had happened for a reason. What that reason was, I lost in the depths of my mind and pain. I realize that I was just as responsible for what had happened to me as were the folks on the dock. In fact, it was beyond all our control; it was meant to happen. At the time, I had lessons to learn and a gift to receive. I later realized the lessons are repeated until learned. I took little consolation in this idea as my struggle was just to get through the next moment of pain that I knew would soon come and did, too often.

Forcing yourself to stay in control is just another form of panic. Much later in my life, I realized this. I learned that it is better to let events move at their own pace than to forcibly intervene. That lesson is something I now remember every day. I discovered that the answer to panic—tranquillity—was within me. Ultimately, the awareness dawned on me that everything happens for a reason.

Ten days later, I was released from the hospital. My left eye was still barely functional, although the scab that had covered the left side of my head had almost disappeared. Physically, I looked okay to the outside world, with the exception of my left arm hanging in a sling. I had no control over it. It was separated from my shoulder by a measure of two fingers, held in place by stretched skin, muscles, sinew and, of course, the sling. The slightest movement would send a dagger of pain through my entire being. Temporarily, I would lose control of myself, grit my teeth and curse. I cursed a hell of a lot!

The walk to the hotel only yards from the hospital exhausted me. I was just getting used to breathing with one lung. My left lung had collapsed as a result of the paralysis on the left side of my diaphragm. There was little the Bahamian doctors could do for me. Their outdated equipment and medical techniques did not allow for much more than their taking a series of X rays, so poor in quality they were of little value, except to show that something had been badly messed up inside my body. My condition was stabilized. I was armed with only a bagful of pills and my prayers for release from the pain. The pills, prayers and Laini were the only things of value to me at the time.

That night, Laini and I had to stay at a hotel. She chose a cheaper one than the one we had been staying at since our stay had been greatly extended, and the costs were mounting quickly. Airline officials insisted I stay at least one night in a hotel before they would allow me to board the plane; otherwise, I would have to take an air ambulance. Fortunately, the doctor had prescribed a drug that dulled some of the pain, enough for me to put up a good facade. The drugs and the desire to be home helped me get through the next 24 hours. By then, I had an aversion to anything or anyone touching my left side. The slightest contact sent shock waves of pain coursing through my side.

Desperately, I grabbed and squeezed Laini's hand whenever I could. It was my one hold on sanity. This simple human contact kept me centered on the task at hand: getting home, seeing my doctor, believing he could fix my body. I was desperately trying to divorce my mind from my body, to little avail. Hope and despair mingled in ever-increasing intensity that night and the following day. The drug-induced sleep was a relief, a prelude to my descent into a living hell.

Home at Last.
Drugs, Booze and Modern Medicine, Here I Come!

Mid-August, 1982

Mom had come in from Montreal to meet us at the airport. She looked visibly relieved when she saw me. To her, I looked basically okay, just slightly battered from my accident. I will always be grateful that at this time my body appeared normal. But inside my body, it was a different story. The atrophy had already started.

Doctor Prober, my family doctor, saw me within hours of our arrival home. I treasure his kind and caring ways to this day. He is a truly compassionate soul, his waiting room always filled to capacity. He is frustrated only by his inability to help others with the limited tools at his disposal. The first thing he did was stop me from taking the pain pills Dr. Kassees had prescribed, and gave me a safer prescription in its place. The Bahamian-prescribed drug is no longer dispensed in Canada, as it causes kidney failure with continued use. It was the beginning of a seductive journey into drugs, a liaison brimming with promises, but at a price I would come to recognize as too high.

I recall my mom walking with me from the car toward the emergency entrance at North York General Hospital as Laini parked the car. The doors to the hospital swished open electronically. I felt like a wreck as Mom guided me to the receptionist, then to a seat.

Dr. Prober had called ahead and they were waiting for me. I barely had a chance to settle into the chair when the emergency room receptionist began to recite a list of questions. The dehumanization of Ken that started in Nassau began again and was to continue for a long time.

"Name." *Clack clack clack.*

"Insurance policy." *Clack clack clack.*

"Birth date." *Clack clack clack.*

"Next of kin." *Clack clack clack.* On and on and on it went. The cold efficiency of the entire hospital seemed embodied in this one person. I wanted to yell, "I am Ken. Help me, please." I knew I would not be heard. I was too numb and too scared to even care.

She typed, asked, typed and droned on for what seemed like aeons but was only minutes. I was beginning to feel more like an object than a person. I tried to answer, between bolts of pain. Tears welled up as I realized the futility of being human. My mom and Laini answered most of the questions. I relinquished this responsibility, since the pain made talking almost impossible.

Without an opportunity to go home and collect some personal belongings, I went straight to a couple of weeks of, "Let's poke, prod and find out what's wrong with this guy." I found that the tendency of the medical community to dehumanize and objectify patients robs them of dignity and will when it is most needed. I felt more like a money machine than a living, feeling person. "Bank of Ken" seemed to be emblazoned on my forehead.

I believe this is the medical professionals' way of distancing themselves from other people's pain. This I can understand and now accept. It is their coping mechanism to help them deal with the traumas they are confronted with daily. At the time, however, I found this attitude hard to accept. Each day I felt more dehumanized and betrayed by the very people, system and institutions that were there to help me.

The doctors swiftly determined the X rays I had brought from Nassau were of little value so they did not know the exact nature and extent of damage to my body. My pain and fear intensified. A dash of reassurance would have been appreciated, but there was nothing with which to reassure me. I would have settled for a little white lie—anything to hold out hope.

A team of doctors started assessing me. The extensive and unknown complications required significant and laborious effort before a full course of action could be mapped out. Dr. Prober was my anchor. He visited me frequently in the hospital and took the time to explain what his colleagues were discovering about my condition. Now I had a neurologist, lung specialist and a host of others working on my behalf.

X rays, needles, pills, spinal tap, more X rays, more needles, more pills, ECG, EKG. The list seemed endless, and for good measure they tested my breathing capacity. Breathing was a problem. Fourteen years of smoking and now only one functioning lung combined to take a heavy toll. Yet, to this day, smoking is the one addictive relationship

I choose to keep. I have quit for two years since, but repeatedly find an excuse to start again and quit again. It's a game I play with myself, a slower game of Russian roulette. I will stop playing this deadly game. Soon.

Two and a half weeks later, I was released into the care of Laini and that of a homemaker who would assist with my daily necessities, until I started functioning more independently. This was the next phase of the medical path my doctors had chosen for me.

The Specialist

Dr. Bay's office was in St. Michael's Hospital. The dim green hallways had been well traveled by many a soul. The building was mid '50s vintage, boxy and devoid of any character, except perhaps for the opaque windowpane door, marked DR. A. R. BAY, M.B., F.R.C.S.(C), an intimidating set of letters whose meaning I did not understand. They lent an air of superiority to the doctor that further dehumanized me.

Laini opened the door to the small waiting room, which boasted three elegant, old-style hardwood chairs. The office was an organized collection of medical efficiency. Light green in color, old wooden desks, two secretarial staff and a receptionist. Definitely the trappings of an important man. The most important doctor for me. His hands held the fate of my left arm.

"Name."

"Health card."

I had grown weary of this list of repetitive questions asked by all doctors' receptionists. I would answer mechanically between the always-present stabs of pain in my left side. After the first few times, I struggled to do it for myself even if the receptionist was impatient. It was now September. Summer had ended with me in one hospital. Fall began with the prospect of entering another one. I was on a merry-go-round of a never ending series of appointments with doctors and other health-care givers. I was searching for answers to my problems, and as long as there was the promise of hope, I would call, write, walk or do anything to get rid of the pain and improve my condition. I was determined to conquer this pain. Yet, the more I persisted, the more I found it conquering me, and the worse it got. The seeds of an addictive relationship with drugs and doctors had been planted. My dependency on the outside world was flourishing, feeding on my quickly fading inner strength and dignity.

Laini and I were escorted into Dr. Bay's tiny examination room.

"Take off your shirt. Here is a gown. The doctor will be with you shortly," was the singsong litany of a mechanical human as the nurse exited the room. I was becoming accustomed to being treated as an object. I was beginning to beat up on myself, and that was a really addictive relationship, all the more frightening because I had begun to enjoy it. Becoming a victim of circumstances is easy in the world of modern medicine. I felt as if my world had turned inside out, and it had. I felt as if I was there for the medical establishment's needs and not my own.

A tall, rugged man in a white lab coat entered, chart in hand. I noticed his long fingers, like those of an artist or surgeon. In this case, he was both. He glanced at me as he continued to read the chart. I had been reduced to no more than a few words on a piece of paper, with some X-ray photos thrown in for spice. He looked up and said, "I am Dr. Bay and you are Ken Vegotsky."

Why was it that none of these doctors seemed to have a first name, I thought, again feeling more like a thing than a person. "Y-e-s," I stuttered as a shot of pain interrupted my thoughts.

"Take your sling off and show me what you can do with your arm." Mindlessly, I did as he asked, winced with every movement, grappling with the sling, the pain and what felt like a surreal situation.

Swiftly he examined my arm and shoulder, recited his list of questions and then said, "Get dressed and wait in the reception area." He left before I realized the examination was over. The definition of Ken Vegotsky had been reduced to an upper torso left side brachial plexus injury. No longer was I a man with a painful injury, but a case study, a medical anomaly and a neurological/orthopedic freak devoid of either sensations or feelings.

Minutes later, Laini and I were ushered into the inner sanctum, and we settled into the doctor's chairs. We waited expectantly as Dr. Bay examined my chart, the X rays from the spinal tap lighted from behind by the glass panel on his wall.

"You've had a brachial plexus injury. It appears that nerves C 4, 5 and 6 on your left side were avulsed at the roots and C 2, 3, 7 and 8 damaged. You're a perfect candidate for an intercostal nerve graft and transplant." He continued speaking but I heard nothing. I was a candidate. My prayers had been answered at last, I thought.

" . . . some of the pain may be reduced when we operate and remove the scar tissue," he continued.

There was hope for relief. I blanked out thoughts of all else. Dreams of a tomorrow free of pain had taken over my mind.

" . . . a nerve from your left leg will be put into your left side. This is meant to help you have some control over your arm . . . "

I'll be able to use my arm again, I thought.

" . . . it could take two years before we know if it works . . . "

Two years. A small price to pay for a working arm.

"I'll schedule you for surgery as soon as possible." A hint of excitement caught in his voice.

His direct manner and extensive experience were evident in the efficient way he handled me. Standing in the hallway moments later, I found myself somewhat satisfied and hopeful. A whirlwind of emotions, thoughts and prayers mingled with my tears. At long last, a foundation for hope.

The operation seemed simple enough. Dr. Bay was going to take nerves from my left leg and put them in my chest. The nerves would grow so that my brain would again be able to communicate with my biceps. It was like replacing a broken steering wheel and column in a car so that the driver could again control the vehicle.

The drive home seemed to fly as I shared my renewed dreams of being whole again with Laini. I talked incessantly in spite of the shots of pain lunging through my left side. My voice was like a roller coaster riding up and down the waves of pain. Talking had become a way to distract myself.

September, 1982

My neurologist, who didn't say or do very much, gave me a copy of Dr. Bay's letter, and excitedly I reread it. My mind had become so dulled by the drugs and pain that I had problems concentrating. So I started asking for copies of everything. This way I could refer to what was being done for me and have the time to think about what was happening. My body was being battered so constantly that I sought constant refuge in sleep. I was being exhausted by the pain at every level, not just physically, but emotionally and mentally, as well. My spirit, too, had suffered.

A friend had lent me a VCR and tapes. The science fiction movies I loved, and even the adult tapes did not keep me awake. A big brown couch from my bachelor days had become my second bed. Nothing, absolutely nothing, stopped me from falling asleep. Except the pain!

I read and reread Dr. Bay's letter between stabs of pain. It was his game plan for my future care. He was the first doctor in the world to perform this particular surgery for my type of brachial plexus injury and was listed as one of the top, if not the top, doctor for the type of injury I had.

My eyes teared over as I read about my past, present and future health care. My prayers and hopes were alive once again.

RE: Kenneth Vegotsky

" . . . we will achieve this by doing an intercostal sural nerve graft."

Looked good to me.

"I will bring him into hospital right away."

Getting better.

"and in the next two years, consider the question of a shoulder fusion and Steindler procedure to the elbow."

Yes! Yes! Yes! I thought, I'll be okay in two years.

" . . . he will be the 150th brachial plexus operative case that I have performed in the last 10 years.

"Best personal regards. A. R. Bay, M.B., F.R.C.S.(C)"

Patient to be admitted September 22, 1982.

I was reading a book about surgery and what could happen. By coincidence, it had been written by one of the staff members of St. Michael's Hospital, so I had an even greater connection to its contents. The facts were not encouraging. For the year quoted in the book, 1600 operations had been done at the hospital, but 3 out of 100 patients had died. Fear took hold of me. I had no plans but decided it was time to reevaluate what was happening.

The medical community is rather tight-lipped about itself. As a patient, I was discovering this rapidly. When it came to surgery, I realized I was handing my life over to someone who would not have to live with the consequences as much as I would. The doctors are gods in the minds of the public and they get to bury their mistakes. I was not comfortable with giving away control of my life, and I discovered they were not comfortable with relinquishing their power.

Already I was on the fifth type of pain pill, rapidly ascending the ladder of medications. None of the pills eased the pain, and each new medication took away a little bit of hope. As each pill failed, my will to live was gradually eroding. Increasing despair and depression were becoming a daily part of my life—more medications, more failures, more pills and a sense of desperation that was almost my undoing. The visits to doctors increased, as did my desperation. The doctors could not do anything for my pain except prescribe a pill and get rid of me. It was a vicious cycle. I saw other people on drugs so strong that they had to give up control over their lives to the side effects of drugs, in an attempt to escape their pain. I was terrified.

Who is it that made this medical machine so powerful?

The question kept haunting me. Today I realize it is you and I who give up our responsibility for our health. The traditional health-care givers willingly accept this gift. It means a life of luxury and a lack of immediate accountability. They are just doing what is asked of them, to make the decisions for us. My seeds of self-empowerment were planted by my fears and they were beginning to take root. Soon they started to grow.

That Fateful Night—The Gift

I pulled on my jogging pants as I battled with shooting pains. My left arm hung uselessly, a constant reminder of the accident. I had been fitted with a custom leather sling to cradle my arm, since it would be years before the surgeons would stabilize my arm—no matter what I chose to do. Another jolt shot through my body.

Putting on the loose-fitting shirt was a frustrating and long exercise in acrobatics and pain. Even the simplest activity was agony. I couldn't take it anymore! Tonight, a friend had offered to take me to a strip joint. I was scared, desperate and had a plan. This was to be my last try at relief.

"Ken, he's here!" Laini yelled from the downstairs entrance.

"I'm coming!" I yelled back. A dagger of pain lunged through my body. I grabbed the pain pills I had been saving—those I no longer took, and a partially filled bottle of the most recent prescription.

Please, God, please help me have the courage to do it, I thought as I clung to the railing and slowly descended the stairs, popping a handful of pills in my mouth and swallowing.

I arrived at the bottom of the staircase and hugged Laini. I planted a big kiss and said, "I love you. Goodbye." I quickly turned, before she could react, and headed out to the crisp fall night and waiting car.

As I opened the car door, I said a silent prayer, hoping my experiment in relief would work. If the drugs, booze and naked bodies didn't work, then the thought of overdosing myself comforted me. Death was an inviting idea compared to living with my pain. The pills were starting to dull my mind. It gets dark earlier in the fall, but the darkness was now inside me, always. It was my perpetual punishment.

The drive to the striptease bar went swiftly. My pain did not lessen, so I kept popping more pills. I savored the idea of alcohol coursing through my veins chasing the painkillers. I had already experimented with pills and alcohol at home, gingerly seeing if it would work to rid me of pain. So far it had not.

But tonight I was going all the way. No one realized what I was doing. No one seemed to care. Doctors gave pills and friends and family gave pity or advice, with an occasional dash of something that might pass for love. My search for outside help was coming to an end. I would not live this hellish nightmare anymore! The pain had robbed me of all I valued, even my will to live.

The Strip Joint

Soon my friend and I were seated at the foot of the stage. The alcohol and gyrating naked bodies in the smoky room had everyone in the crowd mesmerized. Everyone except me. More pills, more alcohol and more attempts at distraction did nothing to lessen my pain. Frustrated, I finished all the pills within the first hour. My pain was finishing my spirit and my soul. More booze! More naked bodies! Nothing worked. The pain rolled on its merciless quest to destroy me. I was drunk and putting up a good front.

The uneventful drive home gave me time to think. I had planned my next move like a coldhearted killer. The victim was to be me. I had given up all hope of having my prayers for relief answered. I had become so detached from the anger, frustration and fears that nothing mattered anymore. Nothing!

Somehow I got out of the car and made my way to the bedroom. It was late and Laini was sound asleep. She had left on the downstairs lights and my bedside lamp.

I stumbled into the bedroom, took off my jogging pants and lay down in the bed. I took one last look at Laini, seeing her in the depths of a tranquil sleep, then turned away. I shut the light as I planned to shut off myself, and I started crying.

God help me, please! I begged as tears of self-pity rolled down my cheek. Please, I pleaded to my unseen self. I can't take it anymore. The pain. God, the pain never ends, please help me end it. The tears became a rainstorm. No one answered. Life is not worth living. I hate myself. I hate the pain. Please help me before it's too late.

Suddenly pain, fear, frustration, anger and a multitude of emotions combined in one instant. I was back on the dock, watching myself floating in the air. The tape in my head played with such clarity that I felt the warmth of the sun, bobbing dock and feelings of horror emanating from the mass consciousness of everyone present. This time, I was an observer. Helplessly, I sat there watching myself as I crashed into the dock, bounced into the water and died. Fear, frustration and anger seized the crowd. I helplessly tried to reach out and stop what was happening. At last I knew the truth. I really had died. The events of my past rested in my mind. At that instant of death, I became one with the universe and God—the universal intelligence. An inner tranquillity took hold of me and stilled my emotions. My mind fell silent. It was the calm after the storm.

Instantly, a warm tingling feeling flowed through my body, mind and soul. A spasm seized the withering body of Ken as he was pulled from the water. I was an observer detached from myself.

The messages came gently and lovingly into my awareness. "You are your own healer. Your mind, body and soul are one with the universe. Accept this gift of love unconditionally. You have a mission in life, that will be done. Let your soul be your guide." I was hypnotized and seduced by these words. They were not my own, but for the first time in my miserable new existence, I found promise and purpose. Exactly what this promise or purpose was, I did not know, but my faith in the universal intelligence was being restored. The journey to my salvation had begun in earnest, at last.

The Morning After

I woke up to a quiet home. Laini had left for work and all I heard were the sounds of the homemaker as she did her chores downstairs. My mind was filled with dreams of huge crowds, laughter and an inner tranquillity that stopped the spasms of pain from seizing control of me. Yes, I had pain, but now my mind had the magic to still it.

For the first time in a long while, I knew I was the master of my destiny. Fate was what I would make of it, must make of it, for I had purpose, a reason for being.

That day, I did not share with anyone what had almost come to pass the night before. It would be years before all the pieces of the puzzle came together. I knew I would face many more tests by fire in the coming years, but at last I was ready to face them.

The Action Plan Evolves

With the new clarity in my mind, I was able to figure out a positive course of action. No longer would I accept the angst, anger and frustrations of those close to me as a basis for dealing with my life. Previously I had had blind faith in others. My newly gained insight into the emotional projections and intellectual processes of other people was key to my inner growth. I was learning to separate the hidden emotional content in words and actions from their intellectual meaning.

Thinking and planning for positive outcomes was comforting. I dreamed of a day when I would be free from pain. I still sensed that something was missing from my life, but for the time being I took on a renewed sense of vigor, and was not compelled to seek the missing pieces. I spent each day contemplating my new plan. I wrote down a few thoughts, and reviewed and added to the list as the day progressed. Sometimes in the morning, to feel useful, I would share my ideas with the homemaker, Diane. One morning, she suggested I make a cake.

It seemed like a fun thing to do, a way of restoring a sense of purpose in my life. All that was required was to make the prepackaged chocolate cake and my mom's special fudge chocolate icing—something I had done many times before, but this time it was different.

"Two eggs, one and a quarter cups of water," Diane said as she placed the electric beater, scissors, mixing bowl and the other items I needed in front of me at the kitchen table. Then she returned to her chores.

It seemed like minutes, yet in fact it took me over an hour to mix, beat and put the ingredients into the cake pans Diane had provided.

I was hungry, and lunchtime had arrived. Quickly I ate lunch, and went to lie down on the couch. I promptly fell asleep.

I was awakened by the childhood smell of fresh-from-the-oven chocolate cake. It was wonderful! It was also the first time in a long time that I woke up feeling refreshed after a brief snooze. I felt great for a moment. Then the pain made a comeback.

"God damn it . . ." I started to say, and stopped my thoughts, choosing to focus on that super special icing. The cake, like my thoughts, had come together rather nicely. All that was needed was a conscious awareness of my goals, and my watering mouth.

Diane laid out all the ingredients and utensils I needed to make the icing and finish the cake. Interruptions for pain breaks were frequent but as short as possible, with the occasional nap thrown in for good measure. A few hours later, the homemaker and I indulged in one heck of a great chocolate fudge cake, without any guilt whatsoever.

Laini was going to be home in a while, so I went to sleep while Diane cleaned up and put the cake in the refrigerator. This cake felt like the greatest achievement of my life. It was a simple way to focus on positive outcomes.

I drifted off to sleep, comforted by the sounds of the homemaker's footsteps as she checked up on me, left the house and locked the front door. It was a peaceful and restful interlude in what was to become an even more painful life.

A Super Evening

I awoke to the smells of supper cooking. Laini can be a great cook. The cake may have promoted a sense of competition in her, because her meat sauce spaghetti suppers are a treat, and that's what I was smelling. I love garlic.

Shots of pain wounded me as I headed to the kitchen. But this time I stopped, grimaced and tried to quiet my mind. It was the longest short walk I had ever taken.

That's it! Deal with the pain. Believe that it is my responsibility. Know that I can. I can! I thought during my trip to the kitchen. I had stumbled onto my main goal for the next nine years.

That night, Laini and I dined like royalty. Garlic-laced meat sauce, garlic bread, soda, and a glorious dessert! Later, I shared my plan of action with Laini.

A satisfied stomach and happy thoughts are a wonderful prelude to sleep. All was well in my world for a brief moment.

The Struggles
No Pain ?! No Gain !?

Sleep was my refuge from my world of pain. My only alarm clock was the daggers of pain that went off whenever they chose to. I had no control over them. One day I kept track of the time and found out I had slept more than 18 hours. My body was telling me something, and during sleep my mind mapped out the plan. I discovered that sleep and my mind were two of my most powerful healing allies.

I was learning to focus on making pain a friend, a lifelong ally. By now, I was entrenched in the cycle of not letting anyone touch my left side, even though I craved human contact. People did not know about the craving and stopped hugging or touching me altogether. I was sending out confusing signals.

Unfortunately, this extended to my physical, intimate relationship; it was becoming nonexistent. I needed hugs and tenderness more at that time than at any other because it reaffirmed my humanness. Without physical contact, I did not feel totally human. Emotionally, it took me years to deal with this. At that time, I coped with it by overeating.

That morning, I realized I had to crawl before I could walk, and walk before I could run again. While going through the morning rituals of brushing my teeth, shaving and getting dressed, I started to write notes to myself on scraps of paper. I felt it was important to have written records of my thoughts as I realized the pain and drugs were greatly affecting my memory and ability to concentrate.

By the time Laini arrived home that night, I had clearly defined my immediate goals, and loosely clarified what my mission in life was. My first goal was to deal with the pain so I could get on with achieving a better quality of life. My vague sense of purpose in life had to do with making the world a better place. I discovered that if I wanted to change my world, I had to change myself.

The Good News—Bad News Stories Begin

"Fate is what you make it," I say. I was beginning to believe, however, that everything happens for a reason. What that reason was, I did not yet know. The disability insurance from my private policy began after the 30-day waiting period, with no problems. Amazingly, I had bought it less than a month before the accident. That is what I call fate, and a belief in the value of insurance.

The government disability pension was another story. A panel of six, in the nation's capital, reviews a mass of documentation, and determines—based on the nature of the injury—if you are disabled for life. No ands, buts or maybes; it must be a lifetime disability where there is no perceived chance of your returning to the work force.

Patiently, Laini gathered the information from the doctors and sent it off to the government office. Finally, I was staring at an envelope from the government. I tore it open and tears of joy and sadness poured forth. Quickly I called Laini and said, "I have some good news and some bad news."

"Give me the good news first," she said.

"I am getting the lifetime government social security disability. Unfortunately, that means they think I am unable to work for the rest of my life," I said.

Finances had not been too much of a problem at the time. Our savings, Laini's job, and my disability insurance made life easy. In some respects, the addictive relationship to money was evolving.

Fortunately, the drain of medical costs was covered by insurance. It was the other costs, such as transportation and lawyers' fees, that started to add up. You have to sue if you want to collect anything. I was suing a business that was a floating dock, thousands of miles away, in Nassau—a small business, with only a small motorboat as an asset. I did not know if they even had insurance. It took a while to get a lawyer and begin the merry-go-round of pay-me-first-then-I-might-do-or-tell-you-something-of-value. Once you get on it, it is hard to get off.

Meanwhile, Laini was building a solid career. The folks in her office were very helpful, and that meant financial support, more money and a little bit of leeway at work.

The Operation—Surgery 101

The day after the spaghetti dinner, I canceled my scheduled September surgery admission so I could get a second opinion. Laini wrote to Dr. Tarzana, a highly respected surgeon who worked in Norfolk, Virginia. We hoped this was far enough away so that I could get an objective opinion. I had become aware of the closed relationship of one medical professional to another and distance seemed to be the safest way of negating it. It took time to get an answer, and in the end it was the same one as Dr. Bay's.

It was now October, and the pain had not decreased. I was again getting desperate, and my will to live had begun to wane. But I refused to turn back to ineffective pain pills. Dr. Bay and the "crapshoot" operation looked very appealing. I called his office and was rescheduled for surgery in November.

November 21 – 26, 1982

My first night, I slept in St. Michael's Hospital hallway. The neurological floor was in a wing of the hospital built in the early 1900s. Its halls were narrow with dark green linoleum floors and pale yellowish walls. I was supposed to be in one of the wards, but they were filled to capacity and I was thankful just to have a bed. The star patients of the floor were those with brain tumors, an immediate life-threatening neurological disorder. They rated two per room. Thank God I was not one of them.

The following day was a jumble of tests, examinations and a move to a ward room. My closest companion was an 82-year-old gentleman, attached to life-support machinery, waiting to euphemistically "go home for Christmas," as his wife and family said. I don't know if he made it, but I know his soul did find peace.

I tossed, turned and writhed in pain all that night. The whirring and clanking sounds of the life-support machinery hypnotized me. Around two in the morning, a nurse came in and had me sign a release. Somehow, the day shift had forgotten to do this all-important piece of paperwork, and I was in no condition to think clearly. I morbidly speculated about the timing and said my final farewells and prayers. "Three out of 100" were good enough odds for me by then; I was desperate. If I was going to die, it was easier to let another person do it for me.

"Wake up," a voice called to me as a hand gently touched my shoulder.

I spent the next hours in a mixed state of fear and anticipation. My mind was in a jumble. All I wanted was to get it over with. Each bolt of pain reinforced my prayers for release, one way or the other. Finally, the orderly came and wheeled me down to the operating room hallway. Laini, my mom and mother-in-law briefly bade me goodbye as I was wheeled past them.

It might be my last farewell, I thought. Tears welled up from inside, but I could not let my family see my fear. It made me feel a little better that the operating room was in a much newer section of the hospital.

I was outside the operating room, writhing in pain and prayer, when the anesthesiologist came to see me. He checked my name band then said, "I'll see you soon in the O.R.," and left.

It seemed like seconds as the intravenous tube pumped its life-comforting chemicals into my body. A masked figure in green hospital garb came to wheel me into the operating room. A pungent odor of hospital disinfectant struck my nostrils as I was lifted onto the operating table. Faces with green-covered heads and masks surrounded me. I was comforted by the precision of the surgical team. I knew I was in capable hands. A voice behind me started to say, "I am giving you something that will help you sleep. Start counting back from 100 and . . . " His words faded into the distant recesses of my memory at around 97.

Ten hours later I slowly regained awareness. I was a mummy, my arm and upper torso tightly wrapped in bandages. A masked face appeared above me saying, "You're fine, everything is okay. We are going to take you back to your room now."

Thankfully, the sentences were short and clipped. I was awake, I was groggy and I was thirsty. I nodded "okay" as my eyes began to focus. Without glasses, it was hard for me to tell if this was a doctor, nurse or angel, but I was feeling very mellow and did not care anyhow.

Shortly afterward, I was whisked from the room into the ancient hand-operated elevator, then into a hallway. The hallway lights hit my eyes as I was wheeled off the elevator and into the short hall. I looked to the side and saw faces filled with relief as I passed Laini, my mom and my mother-in-law.

"How long was I there?" I asked the person taking me to my room.

"Nine hours," came the reply as I arrived back in my room, to the comforting rhythmic sounds of the life-support machinery. "Don't touch the bandages. Dr. Bay will be in to see you soon."

I was beginning mentally to explore my body.

Dr. Bay briskly walked in, looked at me and, in his usual curt fashion, said, "Do not move your arm or remove the bandages. If you do, then the operation may fail. You will have to be like this for the next few weeks until you come to see me." He turned and left, a "no time to waste" man of great intensity and focus. I wanted to talk with him, but his job was done; I was alive, and he obviously had more important things to do than placate me.

Later, I found out that a heart operation usually took about four and a half hours. I was in the operating room for seven and a half hours. An intercostal nerve graft and transplant was not a simple operation. But all operations are complicated if you are fully anesthetized. Being made unconscious is the most dangerous part of surgery.

The time passed uneventfully. With cold efficiency the hospital staff attended to my immediate recovery and I was home, bruised but no worse—or better—for the experience. The shots of pain were still as bad.

The Post-Operation Checkup

Weeks passed swiftly, and I found myself with Laini in Dr. Bay's examination room. I felt like a side of beef as he examined me in his usual detached and efficient manner. Little time was given for questions, and the answers were direct and curt as always.

"You're going to the Toronto Rehabilitation Centre on Rumsey Road and I'll set an appointment up for you in the outpatient clinic. There is very little I can tell you at this point. I'll see you here during the next two years to monitor your progress," Dr. Bay said as he ushered Laini and me out of his office.

The Rehabilitation Center

The staff at the Toronto Rehabilitation Centre had already seen me for a preadmission assessment and made arrangements for me to get a ride there and back daily.

Whenever I started asking questions about my prognosis, the care givers refrained from giving direct answers. My guess was that they were trying to be encouraging, but it was something I never quite accepted, and at first I resented this condescending approach. Later I began to realize the reason I did not get straight answers was that they did not have them, and were trying to cover their lack of knowledge.

It was a game of misdirection that perpetuated the big lie that my body, mind and soul always needed outside help to heal. In fact, for me it is just the opposite, and that is probably the case for most folks. The planted seeds of doubt became my key to accepting the notion that I had to be my own best friend and boss.

It took many years before I fully regained responsibility for my well-being. I visited the rehabilitation center for more than a year. This was an unusually long time for this government-sponsored rehabilitation center. The center had never had someone who had gone through my type of surgery before. Dr. Bay had asked the facility's administration to let me visit the center for as long as possible, and that had helped.

The time passed swiftly at the Toronto Rehabilitation Centre. The Monday to Friday routine was an anchor for my sanity. The purpose of the operation had been to open a path of communication, which is what nerves do, between my brain and biceps so that I would have some function in my arm. That was also the emphasis of the therapy. It is a reductionist style of health care that was contrary to the real world I was discovering, the real world of the mind-body-soul connection.

By treating me as an "arm with a problem," rather than as a whole person, they isolated my greatest assets—mind and soul—from my body. As absurd as that may sound, that is the way I was treated, by parts rather than the whole. This scientific reductionism still occurs in traditional Western medicine. I felt it was something I had to stop from happening to me, but every time I challenged it, the fear of seeming ungodlike would start the health-care giver on a path of resistance. Lip service was given to my mind, and my soul was not even acknowledged during my visits to the center.

A typical day consisted of going to occupational therapy to try to get my biceps working again. I took any twitch or action as a sign of improvement. The stimulation was to help the brain and biceps connect through my newly transplanted nerve. It was long, hard work, and I asked for and got a mechanism to set up at home so I could keep trying as much as possible.

Next came periods of physiotherapy in the gym and pool, and an occasional session with a social worker. The highlight of the day was a light lunch and the midafternoon taxi ride home. During lunch, I had a chance to talk with the other patients and see how medications affected them. It was a comforting time that allowed me to get back some semblance of control. I felt I was progressing and building up my stamina.

During my visit I asked for and got permission to walk the track at the Del Ray Cardiac Center next door. This important step was taken at my own prompting. I knew I needed to exercise, but my head and neck injury and reduced lung capacity made walking difficult. It was tough getting the head staffperson to break the rules to allow this, but I believe it did more to help me than anything else. Although I was a slow walker, each step counted.

The centers accommodated my longer than normal rehabilitation because I started asking all my doctors to request my continued stay. This reinforced Dr. Bay's request. In the meantime, I waited for signs that the surgery was successful. I had no choice but to wait at least the full two years to see if the nerve graft would be successful.

My car license was withdrawn by the government at the beginning of my time at the center. It probably saved the life of some lucky pedestrian because my shooting pains, poor coordination and lack of neck movement made driving too difficult and uncertain. I used the city's disability bus services and taxis. I wholeheartedly focused on the positive goal of getting back my driving privileges.

It slows the process of recovery when others willingly and gladly take your right to think for yourself away from you, at a time when you most need to be empowered. It was a lesson in cultivating dependency that easily repeated itself, more so for the benefit of others than myself. The health givers found it easier to exert control, rather than give it up. My greatest strides were those I initiated and pursued myself. Each accomplishment, from driving to walking, helped me regain a sense of control over my life.

The shooting pains lessened in frequency during this period. I felt that was the operation's main benefit, even though it was not its main purpose. Some of the scar tissue on the damaged nerves along the spinal column was removed, and this promoted some healing—not much, but enough to give me hope.

Chapter 2

. . . And If the Accident Was Not Enough—1983

The year 1983 was tough in many ways. I still had my personal guarantee outstanding with the bank, for the working partnership I had left at the end of 1981. The bank refused to release me from the guarantee I had signed prior to leaving the company. The business was in dire financial straits. Its affiliation with a large retailer was causing the business problems. The 100-plus retail outlets had so much of the company's merchandise, most of it unpaid for, that by default, the retailer controlled it. It was a case of the tail wagging the dog.

More accurately, this hungry monster had devoured the goods, cash and energy of my partners, and this easy-to-sell-to relationship was addictive in nature. This model of building a very close relationship between seller and buyer was the future of the retail business, but its success could undo a successful manufacturer. The lesson here is not to put all your eggs in one basket.

In 1981, every partner in the business had to sign a personal guarantee to the bank for $10,000,000. Early in 1983 I received a demand for payment of that amount.

Then the government of Quebec sent me a letter saying I owed thousands of dollars in back taxes, interest and penalties. I had left the province six years earlier to expand the business in Toronto, and they had found me at last. By then I did not care much; what was a few thousand more? That's when I found out government tax collectors are a law unto themselves.

I had to retain another lawyer, in Quebec, to work for me. Even though I had sent the tax collectors photocopied checks back and front showing that I had paid them, it was not enough. The lawyer said they wanted the original canceled checks. This upset me. What would happen if the checks got lost on the way to my lawyer? Then I would be in trouble. Ten or twenty thousand dollars is a lot of money. It's possible to pay it off, but not without suffering.

I had managed to put away enough money in my retirement plan and had wisely invested in mutual funds that had grown into a tax-sheltered $50,000 by the time I'd turned 30. The government could seize that money and I was using it to cover other expenses—sundries like the mortgage and lawyer's bills.

The lawyer said I was legally in the right; I had paid my taxes in full. The tax department had lost the record of one payment, and I owed a few dollars in interest because I had paid in installments. The tax collectors said they had not been able to find me, and this drove me nuts. I had sent in my new address when I submitted my 1976 taxes, and lived at this address for two years before buying my first house. Why could the tax collectors not find me? How did they track me down after six years? I guess if you do not trust yourself, you cannot trust another, especially if you're a tax collector.

The lawyer cost $100, the penalties and interest were a few hundred more. In my last conversation with the lawyer, he said, "You're right. They are wrong. You can sue them and possibly win, but is it worth it?" I had enough on my plate by that time, and decided it was not worth it. When it comes to lawyers and the law, the only winners seem to be the lawyers. This was a lesson I would keep relearning.

I have discovered good things and bad things come in threes.

The Psychiatrists and the Monkey on My Back

During my convalescence, I discovered that helping my mind was a drug game played by many of the doctors and psychiatrists. The drugs became a "monkey on my back" from which it was becoming increasingly difficult to break free. At times I sought refuge in them, although I knew they were detrimental to my recovery. My thoughts and feelings were reduced to a set of chemical reactions unconnected to my soul. I find it rather miraculous that I survived these acceptable forms of addictive relationships and dependencies.

Some mental health-care givers, however, were effective and guided me toward the power within myself: to strive to survive the health-care providers' incursions into my mind, body and soul. The nontraditional methods were most helpful.

The Psychiatric Roller Coaster

Dr. Bern, a psychiatrist, had written a book about anger, an emotion I had not dealt with. Immediately following the accident, I chose to get on with my life in deed and in fact rather than be concerned with the "whys." I discovered "why" was a useless question anchoring me in the past rather than allowing me to move forward in the present. The physical and emotional pain I was burying under drugs constantly lurked below my consciousness and affected me greatly. I sensed that the key to dealing with the pain was not to bury it, but to allow myself to accept it and envision a better future.

The doctors and drugs masked the problem by not letting the trauma and pain naturally purge my mind, body and soul. Dr. Prober, my family physician, intuitively understood I was angry, and referred me to Dr. Bern. That is when my drug-induced emotional roller-coaster rides became legitimized drug taking. I went from a day tripper to a season's pass holder.

I booked my appointment with Dr. Bern and arranged my disability bus ride to his midtown office. He was located on the ground-floor offices of an apartment building complex. It was a very calming location. If I had to wait for my ride home, it would be a relaxing place to do so. This was my first visit to a psychiatrist after my accident.

Dr. Bern's receptionist was a kind soul, although a tad condescending at times. Her manner seemed to say, "If you have to see the doctor, then remember I am the guardian who controls access to his inner sanctum and waiting room." It was an attitude I could have done without. I was the one with the problem, not her. It was always a bit unnerving dealing with her, but she had her excuse: she was the receptionist and followed the "doctor's orders."

Dr. Bern immediately put me on an antidepressant; considering my state of mind, it seemed like a good idea. The drug failed to alleviate my depression and created another problem—I started getting headaches.

I saw Dr. Prober and complained about a sudden increase in headaches. He asked what new medications I was taking, and I mentioned the antidepressant. He checked my blood pressure and found it was high. Immediately, he reduced my use of the drug to ensure that my blood pressure would go down without the complications of withdrawal. He told me to go back to Dr. Bern, as he was the doctor treating me for depression. This was a prudent approach, especially considering how rapidly my medicine cabinet was filling up with drugs. But none of Dr. Bern's prescriptions was particularly effective for my problems, and my body began to rebel. I felt I was becoming a living lab experiment to test which drugs might work on me.

This is the gist of a conversation with Dr. Bern shortly after I started on the first drug he'd prescribed:

"Dr. Prober thinks the antidepressant caused my blood pressure to rise," I said.

"I don't believe the drug caused that to happen. I'll check your pressure now and watch it more closely in the future," he replied as he retrieved his symbols of power—the blood pressure cuff and stethoscope—from his desk. He took my blood pressure and it was still up, since the body takes time to clear itself of drugs. He informed me that my body had not had sufficient time to adjust to the antidepressant.

It was difficult to sort out these confusing signals: one doctor saying stop the drug, the other saying use it. The mixed messages planted seeds of doubt as the medication continued to assault my body, mind and soul. I felt torn between two conflicting opinions. And the wrong choice could mean my life.

Dr. Bern disregarded the signs and put me back on the pills again. When I went to see Dr. Prober, again my blood pressure was up. He took me off the antidepressant. Back to Dr. Bern I went, and was put back on the drug. This game was becoming a habit as addictive as the drugs. Finally, Laini accompanied me to Dr. Bern's. Her support helped me decide to stop seeing him. But I did not get off the roller coaster; rather, I turned to another psychiatrist.

Chapter 3

The Calm Between the Storms—1984

The year began gently. I had a new psychiatrist, the rehabilitation center was helping me keep focused on my physical recovery and I started going to the outpatient clinics at St. Michael's. The operation had reduced the pain only a little, but I was very thankful for even that little bit of relief. My arm, however, did not seem any better; in fact, it kept getting worse. My breathing had improved slightly as I had quit smoking. I no longer needed a cane to stabilize me, although climbing stairs was very exhausting. My stamina and body were getting back to a state of equilibrium. My mind and the bolts of pain were another story.

The Psychiatrists, the Hypnotherapist and the Monkey on My Back (Continued)

The only thing that stands out in my memory about my new psychiatrist was that his office was located upstairs next to a candy store. Food was playing a bigger role in my life each passing day. Stimulants like chocolate, in particular, gave me a quick pick-me-up. The chocolate-induced euphoria was my body signaling that I was having a mild allergic reaction. The new antidepressants I started taking helped, to a degree, but at a price.

Dr. Vague's methods were the same: listen to me, placate me, put me on drugs and set up another appointment in two weeks. That made my family feel okay. It seemed I was doing something to help myself, and in their minds they could feel passively helpful. The only flaw in this process was that I did not feel more in control of my life or much better emotionally, just outwardly more stable.

I continued to turn my anger inward and became more depressed. The drugs added confusion to my feelings of despondency. I could only count on the psychiatrist not to turn away when I tried to share my feelings, and he did not comment much about them. A feeling of emotional helplessness took hold.

That the psychiatrist listened, albeit passively, made it easy to turn to him. No one else wanted to hear about my physical and emotional pains. All I really needed was a good friend, and so the search for one began. The answer to this quest was surprisingly simple; so simple in fact, I subconsciously kept overlooking it. Eventually, I did find that friend.

Those who I expected to listen, didn't. Friends and family would nod and say, "That's okay," as they politely distanced themselves from my emotional pain as if it were contagious. This made me feel abandoned, and my distress grew and grew.

Increasingly, I felt powerless to cope with my feelings. My sense of abandonment grew until one day I found myself with anxiety so overwhelming, I was incapable of reading the comics in a newspaper.

What had I done? Why was I being punished again? The victim mentality started to permeate all my relationships. I saw that everyone seemed to be addicted to keeping and making other people dependent on them. These relationships of dependency promoted gratification through control. I constantly faced the same dilemma: assert my independence and be punished for it, or victimize myself and be rewarded with people's approval. The emotional pain just weakened my ability to heal and deal with the trauma. My physical pain kept reasserting itself, defeating me more each time.

Laini and I had had the bond of mutual need as the foundation of our relationship. The accident changed my role to one of dependence. Daily I anxiously awaited Laini's return from work as I sat in my recliner, my only comfortable chair.

I slowly started seeking alternative coping strategies that did not involve drugs. I started to see Dr. Maui, a family physician who had given up his traditional medical practice to become a hypnotherapist. More than a year had passed since my accident. I had little relief, and was willing to try almost anything to deal with my physical and emotional pain. The lightning bolts of physical pain fed off the emotional pain, and vice versa. It was a vicious cycle of never ending pain.

I enjoyed my sessions with Dr. Maui and always felt better after them. He used the techniques of positive affirmations through hypnosis. It was my conscious choice to enter a heightened state of receptivity. I began rebuilding my inner self and resolving my problems. Yet I was still on the psychiatric roller coaster.

Pain still grabbed hold of me constantly, but I was finding distractions and sleep worked. Unfortunately, however, I was not sleeping well. Every night, I woke with an incredible burning sensation in my chest. I thought I was having a heart attack each time. Dr. Prober had taken ECGs, and these tests had indicated there was a heart irregularity, but nothing immediately life-threatening. It was minor compared to what I was going through with constant flashes of pain in my body.

"Don't smoke or eat spicy food," he advised.

I quit smoking and stopped eating spicy food, but the chest pains and foul tastes in my mouth would not go away. I had to do something. The chest pain on top of the others was destroying my ability to function. Finally, Dr. Prober sent me to a specialist at Mount Sinai Hospital.

The test was very simple: stick a tube down my nostrils and measure the amount of acid in my system. It was not pleasant, but when you are desperate, you will do anything. I had a very bad case of heartburn, and I was told it was common in cancer patients who'd had a lung removed. When the paralyzed left diaphragm caused my left lung to collapse, my stomach had filled the cavity. My sphincter muscle had weakened, and stomach acids went into my mouth constantly.

The specialist said they could operate on the sphincter muscle, but six months later the problem would probably come back. It would be better if I tried Tagamet, a new anti-ulcer drug that worked on heartburn. Motilium could also be taken if the problem got worse. These drugs did actually work. I could once more sleep through the night, which was when my body and mind did their best healing. My waning faith in drugs was restored.

Now I could eat without throwing up and experiencing heartburn. What a relief it was. I started making up for lost eating time. Food tasted great again. Nothing went to waste, yet that is where it ended up—on my waist, face, arms and legs, thereby creating a new problem. The long-term answer to my problem was not the Band-Aid of food or the Band-Aid of drugs that I had turned to. I felt it had to be simpler than that.

The Bad News

Personal bankruptcy was becoming a distinct possibility. Ten million dollars was a lot more than I could afford to pay off. My retirement fund was being eaten up rather quickly. Laini's car was in the garage on blocks since I could not drive, and that eased the financial drain. Money did not appear to be a problem—yet.

I retained two lawyers: one in Nassau, who did not seem to be doing much of anything, except calling or writing when he needed more money, and one in Toronto to talk with the unresponsive one in Nassau and try to get him to do something. It is very frustrating dealing with a distant legal counsel in a country with a small legal community. Their bar association was no help when I contacted them. I realized I had taken for granted our legal system, and now I started to appreciate it and the merit of its accountability to a higher authority, the bar associations.

The lawsuit had a price, and it slowly chipped away at our reserves—monetary and emotional. But Laini's climb up the corporate ladder meant more money coming in, so we did not feel a financial crush.

My now two-year-old operation was having frustratingly little effect on my arm. I tried all I could to help my arm improve, but the intercostal nerve graft and transplant had failed. It was time to visit the orthopedic surgeon at St. Michael's Hospital.

The Good News

Laini and I desperately wanted to have a child. In my case it was an act of selfishness to reaffirm my existence, motivated by my fear of dying during the next round of surgeries. It gave me hope for a better tomorrow and a sense of purpose.

After many months of trying and running to doctors, the good news arrived: Laini had conceived. She was pregnant. My dream of bringing a child into this world would be fulfilled. Selfishness has its place. My stamina was increasing and that was important, as I feared dying on the operating table. My next surgeries were fast approaching.

My breathing was also showing signs of improvement. The weight I was putting on did not help, but Ventolin and other drugs for the asthma—triggered by the accident and made worse by smoking—seemed to help. Physical activity and stopping smoking for a few months were having positive results.

I found a great masseuse, Tom, at the fitness facility where I swam and walked. Fortunately, health insurance covered this cost. The physical pain had caused me to drive others away from touching me, but I was overcoming this fear. The walk, swim and massage were soothing experiences that allowed me to fill my days with peaceful physical activity that reaffirmed my body's sensations and its abilities to strengthen and heal itself. In the low lights and calming music of the massage room, I could let my mind listen to itself. I was getting in touch with my inner self again as the massage relaxed my mind and body.

Good things happen in threes, and that year I was tested and given back my license to drive. It was a victory for my independence.

The Orthopedic Surgeon

Dr. Rich had the hands of a surgeon and a warm manner that made me feel comfortable. He explained what would be done, an approach which contrasted with the way most doctors had treated me.

"Your arm is going to be fused to your shoulder," he said. "This will give it stability. The Steinhedler procedure will enable you to bend your arm up and down. How much practice bending you do will determine your range of motion."

I had begrudgingly come to accept pain as part of my life, and Dr. Rich offered no possibilities of help in that regard. I found it difficult to carry on the conversation without grimacing, as stabs of pain shot through my side. At least the operation held out hope that I could rid myself of the sling. That would stop people from labeling me as disabled. So much of what people think is based on what they see, which blinded them to the real me.

I knew I had to go through with these operations. Selfishness is a great motivator. I wanted very much to be accepted as a whole person again. The sling and the acrobatics I performed to get dressed were painful. I welcomed the surgeries since I wanted to be ready to see my child and have him or her see me as a complete person. If I could not be whole in the baby's sight, then I preferred to die on the operating table. My pain blinded me. I saw life in terms of black and white, yes and no.

My surgeries were scheduled for the end of January 1985.

Chapter 4

. . . And If the Surgery Was Not Enough—1985

January started with excitement. For the first time, the Bahamian lawyer called without a demand for money. Instead, he had news that the parasailing company had an insurance policy for a quarter of a million dollars and the insurance company wanted to visit me. The timing was less than perfect.

"Sure, I'll be in St. Michael's Hospital undergoing two surgeries. It will be my pleasure to see the insurance people there," I said. It had been over two years since the accident, and at last something positive was happening on the financial front. The fact that I was going in for more surgeries substantiated my problem. In that regard, the timing was perfect, almost as if an unseen hand was acting on my behalf.

I was beginning to believe I had friends, in that other world, helping me. Fate works in mysterious ways. I wondered if my guardian angels had interceded on my behalf. Maybe they had.

The Orthopedic Surgeries

Last week of January – First week of February 1985

Tuesday, January 29, 1985, was a typical cold winter day. Laini drove me to the hospital and accompanied me to the admitting office. Again I was the object of a surgeon's desires. Being an object in a human body is easy if all the players are willing, and I was anxious to get the operation over with, but I was also scared to death that I would not live to see my wife give birth.

43

This objectification awoke me to the fact that my body was in my mind. That thought kept me sane. Friends to whom I tried to explain this would shake their heads as if to say, "That's okay, he's just scared." I was being treated like a child.

The next day I was prepared for surgery. I underwent a battery of questions and tests. Dr. Rich asked if they could take pictures of me since they were going to use an experimental material to screw into my arm and shoulder bones for my shoulder fusion. I was a living experiment. I did not fully comprehend this.

The metal plate they were using was a different material than normal. I was never told the exact nature of the difference. Usually after a shoulder fusion operation, another operation would be performed a year later after the two bones had become one. During that second operation, the metal joiner screwed into the bones would be removed to prevent gangrene.

I was not told about this normal course of events for a shoulder fusion until after the surgery. The timing for this medical advance, and events in my life, was too perfect. I realized my good fortune. This new type of plate would not be removed. I was lucky. Fate was dealing me a good hand.

Thursday, January 31 started with my visit to surgery. The operation went well, but afterward there was a terrible burning sensation in my forearm that would not go away.

An out-of-town friend came to visit me in the hospital. Laini, he and I were talking in my hospital room. The shooting pains, postoperative pain and now this persistent burning sensation in my arm were making it hard for me to concentrate. A nurse armed with a needle came in.

"What's that?" I asked.

"Morphine, to help you deal with the postoperative pain," she said.

"No, I don't want it," I stated, since I had been learning to use my mind power to cope with the pain. The self-hypnosis and affirmations were very helpful only if I had complete control of my mind.

"You have to get your shot," she said. Laini and my friend slowly inched out the door.

"*No!*" I insisted.

Not swayed by my refusal, she gave me the shot of morphine. This external intervention forced my pain to return with a vengeance. I hated the drugs and the people who always claimed to know what was best for me, again and again and again. Years of coming to terms with shooting pains went down the drain with one shot of morphine. The morphine released a demonic world, which was suddenly agony. The shooting pains had their way with me. The medical establishment's attempt at imposing relief caused me to take a step back, into my past, into a world filled with uncontrollable pain. I forgive the health-care givers, for they do not know what they did.

What hurt most was Laini and my friend standing there and watching while I was being raped with drugs. I realized only I would ever be able to take care of my needs, and that no meant *no!*

That weekend, my body, mind and soul rebelled. I was angry and frustrated by these crude interventions without my permission and stood firm with the nurses about blood being taken once a day. It was scary. The nurses seemed like soldiers marching into battle—with me the territory for them to conquer and control.

The hospital routine had a rhythm of its own: dressing my wound and taking care of my minimal needs to sustain me for the next surgery. Shift changes brought a flurry of activity that ebbed and flowed. My pain had gotten worse. Now I wanted relief, which meant sleep. An endless flow of pills, nurses and doctors blended together. My spirits started to pick up by Monday with the expectation of getting the last surgery over with, then going home. Death had knocked at my door often enough for me to know it was not yet my time.

I was concerned that the Bahamian insurance representative had not shown up at the hospital. The lawyer I had retained to communicate with the Bahamian lawyer was a sole practitioner who diligently and knowledgeably pursued his work. His small law firm suited my personality. I called him to find out what was happening, and sure enough, he did not know. I guess the insurance company saved a few dollars by not flying someone in to see me at the hospital but merely called the hospital to see if I was there. Unfortunately, I was.

February 5, 1985

My anxiety vanquished thoughts about lawyers and settlements. I was resigned that I would never get enough to compensate me for my pain, let alone lost income. Money does not make the world go round; it just makes it easier to survive with dignity. The only ones who offered any financial support were my mom, sister and a wealthy cousin.

Fortunately, due to my good financial planning, this help was not needed. My fear of death and concern for my family's well-being was mollified because the year before the accident, I had upped my life insurance. If I died, my wife and child would be taken care of. Those were my thoughts as I looked at Laini, her figure showing signs of pregnancy as the June arrival date moved closer.

The shoulder fusion was my final surgery. The routine of nurses, pills and postoperative morphine shots went as the doctors had planned. In their minds, I was no worse for wear. I kept my thoughts of violation and anger to myself, since no one listened or interceded on my behalf anyway.

It was a hell of a way to learn you are alone in the world—a lesson I angrily dealt with silently. Never again, I vowed to myself. Never again.

Thursday, Laini drove me home. Before I left, an appointment was set up for the outpatient clinic to track my progress.

Oh What a Relief It Is . . .

The business bankruptcy proceedings were two years old. I answered all the bank's questions. They were finally satisfied that legally they could not touch my disability policies or settlement from the accident. Fortunately, our house was in Laini's name. The bank actively pursued my partners from the company, who signed papers allowing the bank to deal with me separately. I appreciated their compassion. At last I could have my guarantee to the bank for the $10,000,000 removed.

It amazed me that my ex-working partner, the president and principal owner of the company, did not lose the use of his Aston Martin or his huge country chalet, and had gained control over millions of dollars of inventory from the now-bankrupt company. I heard that his lifestyle had not changed one iota. He was a brilliant entrepreneur with a grade school education and the shrewdness that comes with having acquired street smarts.

"Do your homework," he kept telling me, and I learned to apply this lesson to life. It was one gift I got from my association with him. I respected and hated him at the same time. These mixed feelings were frustrating.

In February 1985, I was released from my guarantee. The fear of having to declare bankruptcy was removed. My reprieve was contained in a simple letter:

Dear Sir:

Herein find a release from your personal guarantee for the indebtedness of the company, dated April 1981 . . .

The Pregnant Pause

On the surface, life went on; everything seemed to be okay. Winter became spring as Laini blossomed. Thoughts of independence and the freedom the insurance settlement would buy, as well as the purchase of baby furniture, filled my mind.

I had the good fortune of finding an honest and considerate retailer named Alan. He helped put together a package of baby furniture and other things that would make the arrival of our child easier.

Alan's store, Mothers World, offered everything you could want and more. I enjoyed making occasional trips there to speak to him. His brilliant marketing strategies had my admiration and reminded me of my days selling to retailers. An independent retailer struggling to succeed and exploit the inefficiencies of the marketplace was someone I respected.

I told Alan we would become friends. He gently laughed, and told me I would have to be the one to pursue friendship because he was notoriously lazy about phoning. I was hungry to make a new beginning, and people who accepted me for who and what I was became very important to me.

This was a step in the right direction as I distanced myself from those who wanted me to conform to their ways. That did not work for me anymore. I knew I had to take care of myself. That was the lesson I had learned from my last surgeries.

The days were filled with both pain and the excitement of preparing for the baby. Our prenatal classes were an adventure in adjusting to a new reality. The nurse who instructed the classes asked what was wrong with me. I told her about the nerve damage. She could see me grimacing as the pains shot through my body.

She looked at my wife and said, "The pain he has is worse than kidney stones or delivery." That was the only time someone candidly acknowledged how bad my nerve damage pain was. I agreed with the instructor, especially since I remembered having kidney stones when I was a teenager. It had been hell, but like pregnancy, it had passed. My pains from the accident, however, never left.

May 30, 1985

That Thursday started as usual. I made Laini her snack-size meals. I felt useful and enjoyed sneaking lots of good foods, like carrots and apples, for her and the baby into her lunch bag. Up until then, Laini's pregnancy was normal. She was feeling fine, and work as a senior consultant filled her days nicely. This was the last week before her maternity leave began.

Laini left for work as usual. I settled into my morning routine of planning for a day of coping and resting and arranging some things for Laini that weekend. Suddenly Laini was back home.

"I started getting labor pains on the way to work, and stopped at the doctor's office. He gave me an internal, said everything was okay and that I should go home and rest," she said.

I discovered this was the way doctors said nature is a great healer, if you give it a chance.

They spoke in codes that reinforced their status, and I found myself giving in to this desire to go to doctors and have them tell me what I already knew. Laini found herself in the same situation. It is a subtle way that health-care givers make children out of adults, and we seem to want that pampering. The doctors are the winners with this approach. Their paychecks grow bigger the more dependent we act. I was becoming aware of these addictive relationships and how I empowered them.

An internal examination at that point in Laini's pregnancy almost guaranteed she would go into labor and she did. The false labor pains turned real within the hour. Off to the hospital we went. I had a cassette player and soothing music ready for Laini's bedside.

The delivery and maternity areas are the nicest parts of hospitals. Good things happen there. Laini was given a private room where she could labor in peace. I had the job of being there for her. Laini is rather stoic and private, so she kept kicking me out as she moaned, groaned and writhed in pain. I could relate to this.

The moment of delivery grew closer and the nurse came in and asked," Do you want an epidural?"

"No," said Laini.

Our homework indicated that the relief from an epidural was not worth the risk of incurring distress to the baby and Laini. I was despairing of the way health-care givers quickly dispensed drugs with little thought to consequences beyond the immediate ones.

Pharmaceutical companies did their job by making products available. Doctors played their part by instructing people to use drugs even though they were not always called for. Laini and I had come to expect that whenever we went to the doctor's office, a prescription would be presented as the answer to our problems.

In theory, the approach should work, but in fact, it was being abused as a way of keeping the patient happy. It was fast, easy and cost-effective to fill out a prescription. Patient and doctor had become involved in a dependency relationship. No quick fixes might mean you switched doctors. I knew there was something wrong with this setup, but I did not fully grasp what it was.

Hours passed and Laini's labor pains escalated quickly. Suddenly I found myself in a cubbyhole-size change room. Since I had put on over 30 pounds, it was a struggle to get into the hospital pants. The pain was so great, I battled with my sling and useless arm to put on the shirt. The nurses helped me finish dressing. I made it into the delivery room, just in time.

"It's a girl!" the masked doctor said as the nurse took the baby from the doctor, cleaned her and put her on Laini's chest. I felt so good, my body tingled. It was exhilarating.

The baby had a full head of black hair. We were moved from the delivery room to the recovery area across the hall.

Now the fun began. I took 36 pictures in what seemed like minutes. Yeah for automatic Canon cameras! The tingling I felt in the delivery room stayed with me. My pain temporarily abated.

The telephone company benefited as long-distance calls went out to the new grandparents. Stephanie Ali Vegotsky became a wonderful reality.

I was ecstatic and sad at the same time. I felt I would never be able to give my child a real two-armed hug. Tears of self-pity welled up in me as I talked on the phone. They were mistaken for joy by others. That pain, more than anything else, really hurt.

Good News—Bad News (Continued)

The summer and fall of 1985 were a fairy-tale existence. People coming and going, fawning over Stephanie. Laini and I savored the time together.

The first night we put the baby in her own room, she started to cry around midnight. I had not gone to sleep as my pains kept me up most of the night. I went into her room and gently reached in and held her to my chest. Juggling the baby in one arm was becoming second nature to me. Stephanie cried until the morning sun had risen as I rocked through the night with her in my arms. I thought I was calming her, when in truth I was keeping her awake.

The next day, I realized my response to her cries was based on the belief that a parent should do something. Ignoring her would have made me feel guilty. I consciously chose to deal with my child differently in the future and not repeat this subconscious guilt-based routine that the world imposes on parents. Changing my approach took a lot of willpower, since I would have to put up with a lot of criticism. Everyone is quick to judge others' parenting ability, especially if it is contrary to their methods.

I learned to rely on my own thinking. I began to question the model of child rearing that was based on guilt. The seeds of living consciously in the present had been planted. I was living with the consequences of this awareness. Not all of them were pleasant.

By year's end, Laini started working again and our fairy-tale existence was replaced by a routine for her of taking care of the baby and me. She welcomed the dependencies, and fostering this need brought her satisfaction. I was physically and emotionally victimizing myself, but that was easier to do than to resist.

Laini and I found a wonderful child-care provider who worked out of her home. My recently returned driver's license gave me independence. Child care meant I could keep my routine of going for therapy and to doctors. Actually, I was filled with feelings of inadequacy and fears that I could not handle Stephanie alone. What if I could not pick her up for some reason? What if there was an emergency? I had to deal with these anxieties or I would never progress.

I challenged myself daily to take positive actions to deal with my fears and anxieties. I refused to allow myself to give up. I took a CPR course one weekend. The instructors had never before dealt with a person who had only one functioning arm and I challenged their traditional teaching methods. The bottom line was that I could not properly do CPR.

I was dealing with a world of people who did not realize that my arm's inabilities were the small stuff; it was the pain and internal fears that were crippling me. Again, people used only their eyes to determine what was real for them. It is a shallow way to look at life and other people, but it makes it easier for most people to live their lives. They do not have to question their actions. People's misperceptions take the pleasure out of life and build walls between their feelings and interactions, instead of building bridges.

The Bahamian insurance company finally decided to pay me the full value of the policy as settlement, without going to court. But much paperwork had to be done. Like most matters where lawyers are involved, it went slowly, by the clock. This was definitely not to my advantage.

A quarter of a million was a lot of money but I gladly would have given it all away to get rid of the physical pain. I would have given away all my worldly possessions to get rid of the pain. This almost came to pass, but for another reason.

Laini and I decided to move to a bigger home. The first house was paid off with the proceeds from my cashed-in retirement funds. Laini's income had risen sharply as she achieved middle-management status at work and gained more responsibilities in her expanding area. The money was there so we took a risk and made the leap from a small home to a 3,000-plus-square-foot executive home in a good neighborhood. Others thought the move was extravagant, but we felt we could afford it. It was a lucky and timely move. By the time we moved, greed made the world go real estate crazy and we could not have afforded to buy our new home at the higher prices.

The Christmas holiday was wonderful—a trip to see the grandparents, family and friends in Montreal and to show off the baby. The year 1985 turned out to be great. I felt others were watching over us, and they were.

Chapter 5

The Year of Good Fortune—1986

The year started off on a happy note. The settlement for the accident was on its way. The baby was healthy. I was taking back control of my life and planning for the future. The insurance company rehabilitation representative was guiding my steps toward independence. All was well, it seemed.

Preparations for Discovery

Spring was rapidly approaching. The day care for Stephanie was working out just fine. Laini won a gold medal for an accounting exam and was graduating as an accountant. As a woman, she was still a minority in the world of accounting, and an oddity in terms of her achievements in the accounting firm. The money for my settlement had not arrived, and plans to finance a considerable mortgage on our new home were made.

Winter had been a time of further advances for me. The more I did for myself on my own initiative, the less my pain affected me. I made an exciting discovery: the best help I could get started within me. I had learned who my best friend was, and hired myself!

Risk—taking chances—is a four-letter word that means I love me. Armed with this knowledge, I began to take on volunteer jobs to continue my reintegration into society's mainstream. Learning to set goals and plans for the move helped me focus clearly on the processes

I needed for fulfilling myself. I was building a better future for my child, wife and most important, for myself.

In March, the money came through. The lawyer in Nassau received more than $30,000 for doing what appeared to me to be very little. My legal bills in Canada amounted to more than $10,000, so that left me with a little over $200,000. It was a lot, but not enough to make me lose sight of the fact that I wanted to get back into working. I realized work was a privilege I greatly missed. It was play for pay.

Meanwhile, the packing, moving and setting up of the new home took a lot out of me. Constantly, I did things that worsened my pain but I would not give up. A rocking horse for Stephanie, which took me a year to build, was the best piece of furniture in the new home, as far as I was concerned. I assembled shelving, hung pictures and enjoyed puttering around the house.

Dropping Stephanie off at day care and going for exercise and massage helped me immensely. Researching and investing the proceeds of my settlement was a rewarding experience that helped me strengthen my mental abilities which had suffered from lack of use. I had used mutual funds as an investment vehicle since I was in my early 20s; they removed me from the impulse to try to make a quick score. I had done a lot of practical research on them.

I learned that time was an asset that worked for me with my money, just as it did for my recovery. Investing was a hobby that had turned to a passion. The best part was that by my using mutual funds to invest my mom's money she gained her financial independence. When my dad died in 1976, he left her with a very small estate, and she started working full-time as a secretary. The job had helped fulfill her, and it was an example I learned from. Independence and thinking for myself became the thrust of my goal setting.

Inward Turns Outward

Summer became fall, and I got involved in volunteer work. The projects were fun and not too demanding. I sat on the board of the North American Chronic Pain Association of Canada, an affiliate of the American Chronic Pain Association. I had discovered that the best way to deal with my pain was to make a difference with others who suffered similarly. My focus switched from inward to outward. The more I focused outward from within, the less my pain affected my daily living. That was an earth-shattering discovery, one that had beneficial consequences beyond my wildest dreams. I sensed I was doing what had to be done, even though I was not consciously aware of this.

At one board meeting, it became evident that the group needed a federal charity registration, but between the lawyer, doctors and layperson volunteers, no one offered to lend the funds. That night, Laini and I decided to lend the organization the $1,000 needed for the law firm to do the work involved. The fees were a gift on their part.

It was risky, but I had such abundance in my life, I felt I could repay a little bit of what I owed society. Making a difference matters to me.

I figured that each action I turned outward increased my sense of inner harmony and slightly decreased the effects of my physical pain. I began to think more about the gift of life I had been given, the trials I had faced and my unseen guardian angels. The more I focused outward on doing good, the more my body would tingle inside. It acted like a compass; when it points north, you can more clearly decide what path to follow. The path seemed to move farther and farther away from traditional medicine toward nonintrusive health-care choices.

The Psychiatrist, the Hypnotherapist and the Monkey on My Back (Continued)

I felt like a bouncing ball, constantly changing psychiatrists. I finally found one in 1986, Dr. Ikant, who actually talked with me. Psychiatry is more an art form and matter of personalities than a science. His manner suited mine just fine. By the time we met, I had been on numerous types of antidepressants. One was finally working and I was dealing with my depression and anxiety.

Four years of depression was enough. I came to terms with the fact that part of my body was dying before my very eyes. I discovered pain is a crisis that could help me become a better person and that I wanted to be whole again.

Good News—Bad News (Continued)

It unnerved me to see my arm atrophying, and by 1986, four years after the accident, my once firm biceps had turned to a mass of jelly and the skin on my left hand felt soft and smooth, like a baby's bottom. The arm had pain, and my left hand had areas that were numb and always hurting. It was so numb I accidentally dropped part of a hot coal on it and did not realize it until I smelled my flesh burning down to the bone. I was learning the hard way that I had to examine my left side visually to make sure it was not infected or damaged. By age 35, osteoporosis due to the nerve damage had taken hold in my shoulder area, so even a small fall could badly damage me.

The good news was that there was no big bad news that year.

Chapter 6

The Struggles Begin Again—1987

The year 1987 began wonderfully. I had started to do volunteer work at a community dating service and at a clothing manufacturer. I had to learn to get dressed more suitably for the outside world. Five years of wearing only jogging pants and loose-fitting tops came to an end. As I started to show the outside world that I had changed, it began to change its attitudes toward me. I discovered that if you want to change others, you have to change yourself.

This approach worked. Simply focusing on positive outcomes produced positive results. I decided that my positive words, deeds and thoughts were the key to my future prosperity. Once this philosophy was applied, I sensed, everything would come into focus more quickly. The insurance company's rehabilitation consultant helped foster this notion. At first I was suspicious of the insurance company's motives, as it was the money, not my well-being, that it was probably most concerned with. Then I realized that the "why" of the company's motivation was like the "why" of my accident—irrelevant. What mattered was that I make the best of the opportunities offered me, and that's what I was doing.

The Psychiatrist, the Hypnotherapist and the Monkey on My Back (Continued)

Dr. Ikant had a more sharing style than the other psychiatrists. He reflected my thoughts back to me. I broke the cycle of self-pity to find myself with a full-blown case of anxiety. It almost paralyzed me. For many months the anxiety held me in its grasp, but finally I broke free of it. I now had a psychological dependency on drugs, however, and that was something I struggled to conquer.

The self-hypnosis, affirmations, hypnotherapist, family doctor and psychiatrists helped. The hypnosis had the greatest immediate effect. I believe the antidepressants assisted Mother Nature, but it is also possible that they prevented my body and mind from doing what comes naturally—healing.

I started going for massages once a month. The neglect of my body was evident, as I had put on a tremendous amount of weight. I did not want any pictures taken of me. I realized that I would have to deal with this problem, but felt I could delay it until I came to terms with my pain. That meant thinking and planning for weight loss and building my stamina to the next level so I could walk without panting. The more I read, the more the focus switched from weight loss to thinking about my lifestyle. I needed a job or business to fill my time.

With money and time on my hands, that became the next focus and folly.

Good News—Bad News (Continued)

The good news was Laini was pregnant again. I made a conscious choice and prepared to remove a major addictive relationship by discontinuing my government disability pension and to start working again. I felt confident about myself—maybe a little too confident.

I was handling even the bad news, events and pain in stride. I realized that the bad news and events were to build a better me. They were like weights to a weight lifter; they help build muscles.

I was now taking over $1,000 worth of drugs a year, and no pain pills. That was good and bad news, because the drugs affected my memory and body.

I again discovered that things come in threes, and 1988 was going to be a great year, it seemed.

Chapter 7

The Year of Living Dangerously. I Could Fly Again—1988

A business opportunity presented itself early in the new year. A gentleman who had test-marketed a car inspection business in Ottawa was looking for an active partner who had money. The Lemon Detectors, a car inspection service, was born. It meshed with my evolving philosophy of making the world a better place in which to live.

Unfortunately, I started having psychological problems from the stress of the business and from the antidepressants I was taking. The landlord who rented my partner and me a unit in his building misled us about the zoning. I believed I could run a car inspection business from this building since numerous other garages were located in the same building. It was impossible to find legitimate space for an automotive business. The landlord knew this and demanded $10,000 in cash for the lease.

At city hall, I registered the business and found out we were illegally operating an automotive business. I had sunk a considerable amount of time, energy and money into the venture and was not prepared to give up. I knew it paid to cut your losses, but emotionally I had too much invested in the enterprise.

My integrity did not allow me to withdraw the application to operate the car inspection venture. I reasoned that if my business had to do with honestly appraising the condition of a car, then its foundation must be firmly entrenched. My honesty and integrity pushed me over the psychological edge from normalcy to a living hell. This caused me to feel invincible, which was exactly the opposite of how I should have felt.

On May 8, 1988, Alan Scott Vegotsky was born. Now I was the proud father of two, a boy and a girl. All seemed well in my world. I had started writing lots of stories and even copyright registered a book called *The Celebration Of Life*.

However, definite signs of a psychological problem were appearing. Doctors, friends or family neither knew what to do, nor could they identify the problem. Dr. Ikant, the psychiatrist, saw me regularly, and even he did not realize the state I was in.

I was scared to death, confused, illogical and had lost all sense of proportion. I was flying again and, as with my accident, the devastation touched many people directly. I had a full-blown case of something, but I did not know what it was.

Laini lived in fear. She saw our nest egg disappearing as I spent money recklessly. The combination of pregnancy, giving birth, raising Stephanie, dealing with me, running a house, working and all the other "administrivia" of life had taken a toll on her. Our relationship started dying a slow death.

Meanwhile, my tenacity and integrity in refusing to live a lie, and insisting that the city accept my car business application, got a full page article in the *Toronto Sun*, May 24, 1988. The headline read "SOUR LEMONS" by Jerry Gladman. I gave away car inspections and kept fighting city hall to stay open. My partner disappeared. I blew over $200,000, the bulk of my settlement from the accident. It happened so quickly, the sudden realization was too much for me. I fell apart.

The Psychiatrist, the Hypnotherapist and the Monkey on My Back (Continued)

Laini spoke to a social worker who thought I had a case of mania. I remember the look on Laini's face the day she told me this. She was scared. Stephanie and Alan were at her side. There was a tremor in her voice and she couldn't look me in the eye.

"Kenny, I believe you are having a manic episode," she said.

I looked at Alan in the carriage, then at Stephanie. We were standing outside the house. It was a safe place.

"Either you go to the hospital or . . . " Her voice trailed off as the fear of how I would react hit her.

I was relieved. At last I had the answer for my sense of chaos.

Immediately, I drove to the hospital emergency room and admitted myself, thankful at last that I knew what was wrong. The doctor admitted me on the spot. Something was being done.

The psychiatric ward is a world all its own. The staff did their best to deal with a wide range of patients. Some were violent, others had breakdowns and many, like me, needed a haven and time to heal. First, they took away all my drugs. That meant no more antidepressants.

Next, they started me on a course of drug treatment with lithium. Ancient Greeks had used this powerful naturally occurring salt to enhance their moods. I was stabilized and within a few days I began to function normally. Unfortunately, the damage was done.

Dr. Granite, the psychiatrist, met me at the hospital, and took me on as a patient after I was discharged. Drugs are okay for some things, but I kept discovering my fear of them was well-founded. They were too easy to abuse, and doctors, family and I manipulated my use of them.

This was not the way I wanted to live. Drug dependency was slowly killing my mind, body and soul.

I had to break free of this vicious cycle of drugs and doctors. Of key importance is finding a real friend, but when you're on drugs there is a mini-crisis in your body that means you will always need a doctor to monitor you. A friend can help, but it isn't enough. All this was becoming evident to me. Drugs had put me in the hospital, and now they were saving me. Drugs were not the safe and natural choice for maintaining my life.

My world had shattered and fallen apart, again.

Good News—Bad News (Continued)

The small steps forward I had taken came with a price. I paid for the positive events and steps made—I paid with money, my marriage and my sanity. That summer, I closed the business. Emotionally, I felt okay, yet I knew my marriage had suffered a major blow.

Laini and I sought help through a community counseling service. Instead of dealing with the emotional and physical pains, we masked them. We knew we had to do something, but counseling was not the complete answer. Maybe if we sat and talked. Unfortunately, the aftershocks of my mania made that impossible for us to do. That summer, we focused on the house, the children and picking up the pieces.

I did not enjoy bowling, walking or any physical activities. I escaped into science fiction, television and movies. The pain made moving uncomfortable. I wanted to hug the kids so badly with both my arms, and felt inadequate giving them my one-armed and painful-to-me embrace. Food replaced physical satisfaction. I enjoyed eating and put on more weight. The medication worked to alleviate the heartburn, but I still had moments of great discomfort. Sleeplessness was becoming a problem, I thought due to the problems of my business and illness. I began a routine of staying up until two or three in the morning. To the outside world, all was okay, but I knew better.

I needed to start using my mind in a positive way rather than dwelling negatively on the past. My accident and rehabilitation had taught me this. The piercing bolts of pain never stopped, but I was dealing with them by thinking and gently massaging my thoughts, and breathing deeply when they struck. My body's sensitivity to the environment, evident during particular thunderstorms, wreaked havoc, causing my pain to increase greatly.

Real estate school appealed to me as a healthy distraction to take my mind off my pain and suffering. I knew from my accident that setting positive goals benefited me and those around me. It was the best way to deal with the feelings of violation and lost innocence, as well as to earn back some of the $200,000 I had sunk into the business.

That fall I signed up for a real estate course. A bright new future awaited me.

Chapter 8

A New Beginning—1989

The real estate course challenged my mind. I felt whole again. I made new friends to fill the void created by those who drew away from me. The withdrawal by these old friends and family hurt. Even though I dealt with my problem, they preferred not to talk about it or even acknowledge its existence.

The victim role was nothing new. I had to break the cycle for myself if I wanted to survive. I was desperately striving to survive and thrive using what life's journey had thrown my way.

But was my accident chance? Fate? The memories of my near-death started again. I tried to talk to family and friends about it.

I loved myself and knew that self-discipline and a clear focus could overcome adversity. I was plagued by nagging thoughts of incompleteness and a sense of not feeling 100 percent okay. I sensed I had a mission.

Greed! Greed! Greed!

Real estate is a funny business. I had succeeded in sales before, and I was going to succeed again. It was exciting at first. Meeting people, working late, getting going each day. My commitment and enthusiasm were there. I did everything by the book: marketing, making calls, meeting potential clients. I worked hard and discovered this had no bearing on my returns. People did not want a salesman who knew the technicalities, loved selling and loved people.

They wanted words from books that gave the facade of success. They wanted a sales representative who assured them he could get the most money for their house, with the fewest problems, in the shortest time. The most money was whatever the seller wanted; reality said if the house had too high an asking price, it would sit on the market. Time and again I saw homes priced too high that had to come down in price before they sold.

"Mine is worth more, a lot more and what I want to buy is worth a lot less than what they are asking," was the thinking. Self-deception is a fine art that lots of folks practiced. People would string you along, making promises, playing games and hiding behind their words and rationalizations. The concepts of value and price mingled with greed are powerful motivators.

I loved relationship selling based on my principle, but at this time it was not a successful formula for me. When I said "Hi!" I meant Honesty and Integrity. That was not what people wanted. I stayed at my first real estate office for a year and then switched.

The economy had begun its descent into a depressing recession and the greed that motivated most folks came back to haunt them. Bankruptcies, foreclosures and abandoned homes grew to epidemic proportions. The reality was worse than the media presented. I made a living but was not happy.

The Psychiatrist, the Hypnotherapist and the Monkey on My Back (Continued)

Dr. Granite suggested I stop taking lithium. He felt the manic episode was an unusual event brought on by certain things. Since I had experienced only one such episode, I agreed and went off lithium. I told Laini and my mom. They were so afraid, it shocked me. I called Dr. Granite after one week and told him I had started taking the lithium again, and why. Fear of others made me feel like a basket case.

Dr. Granite understood what had happened and kept monitoring me. I could not kick my dependency on drugs, no matter how I tried. Laini, my mom and the outside world imposed their fear on me and I allowed it to affect my decisions. The main difference was that the time between doctor visits increased. This was a good sign.

My hypnotherapist and self-hypnosis techniques worked wonders on strengthening my sense of self. I began to feel in control of my mind. But my body had a mind of its own, fueled by fat-laden processed foods and meats.

Good News—Bad News (Continued)

I found a masseuse near home whom I could afford. Massage had replaced sex, touch and a host of other wants and needs. My body loved being rubbed, and my fear of being touched disappeared. That was the good news. Unfortunately, Laini did not like to do the touching.

Desire was turning to hunger. I was starved for unconditional hugs. I needed something, and massage was only a partial answer.

My thoughts, pains and frustrations went unheard. I felt frustrated at work, home and play. I began smoking for the physical stimulation. My pain only got worse.

The good news is that I started on the road to making a living again. Money makes life easier but not necessarily better. I realized my happiness was defined by how I felt, not by what I earned or owned.

That Christmas, I took my family to Montreal for a vacation. It was time to renew old acquaintances.

Never, Never, Never Give Up!

I connected again that Christmas with Glen, a friend since grade school. His successful better-quality men's clothing store, Henry Marks, was feeling the pains of the recession. Everyone was. He had closed stores, redefined his business and consolidated it in a new location. Surviving these bad times was success enough for most businesspeople. Glen's model was a guide for me. Never, never, never give up!

The economy had fallen off a precipice and interest rates kept rising. Layoffs and major bankruptcies made headlines. The news brought fear of the unknown and talk of a depression. Mass hysteria had hit the real estate market. Many homeowners defaulted on their mortgages. Banks took over the homes, so forced sales started climbing. The greed that fueled the real estate boom had turned to a fear that fueled the flames of economic chaos.

Laini achieved the highest position any woman had held in the 175-person consulting area of the accounting firm for which she worked. This promotion put her at the point where her next step was partnership. Her salary reflected her success. I was bringing in some income from my real estate sales, and financially, life was comfortable.

The Psychiatrist, the Hypnotherapist and the Monkey on My Back (Continued)

Dr. Granite and I had our appointment every three weeks. He felt I should go off the lithium as soon as I was ready. Up to that point, my body tolerated the possible adverse effects of the drug. I read the descriptions of every drug I was taking, and was shocked to learn that all drugs have possible side effects. The difference between most drugs in the pharmacies and the "natural" drugs from health food stores was that prescribed drugs came with studies discussing side effects noted by the patients and doctors. Most of nature's naturally occurring drugs, like essential oils, vitamins, herbs, spices and natural unprocessed food, did not have generally known, verified scientific evidence of negative or positive effects.

Did that make them more dangerous? Why did people resist natural healing drugs and foods? Evidence of intentional ignorance started mounting as I dug deeper and deeper into the motivation of doctors and pharmacological companies. I understood the medical and business motivation as a combination of money-making mechanisms and the masses empowering others to think for them. It is easier to do business with a public that blindly accepts what is done for and to them, at any price.

Doctors made their patients feel they were being helped by receiving prescribed drugs. The pharmacological industry reinforced this perception by trading on the public's fear of the unknown, plus its desire for a quick fix. I wanted the monkey on my back to shake loose. I wanted to stop using the prescription drugs.

Dr. Maui used his gentle hypnotherapy at our biweekly sessions. I felt more centered as I applied the lessons I subconsciously learned at those times. Occasionally, the positive thoughts and words from a tape I heard, years before, replayed itself in my head. Now I started to play life-affirming cassette tapes in my car and at home. They comforted me greatly.

Regular massages eased the discomfort of my body. But physically, I was a wreck. My body was rebelling against the abuses of drugs and processed fat-laden foods. I woke up tired every day. Naps helped but did not solve the problem. My breathing on the one lung worsened and I would sweat profusely or pant at the slightest overexertion, even walking up a flight of stairs. Something was wrong, very wrong.

Good News—Bad News (Continued)

The bad news was my body's rebellion against my lifestyle and condition.

Laini's company merged with a larger major accounting firm as a survival strategy. The government changed regulations for the area of accounting she specialized in. That meant demand for her skills would decrease significantly in the coming years. The writing was on the wall.

The good news was I became aware of my body, and realized I had problems that I could deal with. My mind was more focused and a veil was lifting. I survived another year.

Chapter 9

The Search Continues—1990

Stephanie began kindergarten and Alan was experiencing the challenging twos. In Stephanie I saw my wife growing up; in Alan I saw myself growing up the way I wished I had.

Laini started her own business. Her years of experience and credibility earned her a solid foundation of clients.

My real estate career achieved its goal of getting me back on my feet, but I still lacked the close human contact I needed. The money did not compensate for the long hours, evenings and weekends I worked. My life belonged to potential clients and customers who begrudged me whatever I earned. I realized I could not change the people, so I had to change myself. I made a plan to deal with my problems. The traditional approach of blaming others for my dissatisfaction did not work.

I had a focus. The nightmarish reliving of my death had turned to an acceptance of the messages I had received. My death had happened, and I knew no one wanted to hear me talk about it. Dwelling on the negatives did not get me further, so I got on with life. Sex was a problem. Feelings of inadequacy from the lack of physical contact added frustration and stress to my life. The lack of hugs and kisses made me feel divorced even more from my physical being. My mind and body neither understood nor cared about why this happened. My mind and body cried out for attention, for unconditional love.

My family and Laini's family had an unwritten rule—conform or suffer the consequences. Their way was withdrawal of communication and intimacy.

It could not be their way or I would wither and die inside. I was not going to allow them to treat me like a possession or animal to be

71

trained or cajoled, I defiantly thought to myself. My tenacity came to my rescue.

"Do Your Homework"

I was up late, as usual, watching TV in the family room. Everyone was asleep, and the house was quiet. Suddenly everything turned black. Rather than exciting me, the silence of the night calmed me. I felt a warm comforting tingling in my body. My mind suddenly awakened, and I could swear someone was talking to me. The voice sounded unearthly.

"Who's there?" I asked. Gentle thoughts caressed my mind, "Your mission . . . Do your homework . . . All will be well . . . " I felt possessed by this voice, yet I was in complete control of my body.

I am not crazy, I thought.

My body tingled, and a sense of well-being enveloped me. I got up, went outside and looked at the heavens. I felt compelled to be close to nature. Then it hit me: the answers were all around me. Nature held answers; it was up to me to uncover them. I had to take full responsibility for my life and discover the abundance nature held.

The tingling strengthened as my thoughts clarified my priorities: "Take care of your body. Take care of your mind. Take care of your soul," the wind seemed to whisper.

"You have a mission, follow the path." The pain I constantly lived with changed its nature as if guided by an unseen force. Awakening to the natural power of God—the universal intelligence—was a scary process, after all I had been through. Change had been the only constant in my life and now it was taking me in a new direction.

"What path?" I called into the night sky.

A cold wind touched my body, and the blackened sky turned luminescent as streetlights came alive. I do not know how long I stood there. I only know I had found a taste of inner peace and tranquillity, something I had not felt for a long time. That night I slept deeply. At last I knew I was getting closer to finding my purpose for being, my mission.

The year came to an end with a sense of inner resolve to keep the best, seek the rest and junk the noises and distractions. I had a sense of purpose and that was all I needed.

Chapter 10

The Flood
of Knowledge—1991

"God damn it, what the hell is wrong?" I yelled. Laini responded with silence. She had chosen this way to deal with our relationship. I had chosen a vocal way. Neither approach worked. We were caught in a spiral of frustration and anger. I resolved to deal with my past. My dad had been a "yeller." Determined to break the pattern, I joined a course dealing with anger at a family community service.

My sense of purpose began as a process of centering my ill feelings and dealing with them constructively. Yelling was not an answer. It only increased my physical and emotional pain. I resolved that the feelings of abandonment, rejection and confusion that had guided my life would no longer do so.

I reaffirmed my self-love and self-discipline by repeating to myself, "I love myself and am self-disciplined." Change occurred when I used my imagination to guide myself consciously in the direction I had chosen. Then I realized my direction may have been chosen for me. Fate is what God, the universal intelligence, offered. I realized that fate is what you make of it. I could choose to make what had been offered into a positive result.

The three-month course on anger helped me focus on outcomes. At the end of the course, I was invited to share with others my method of anger control. I was allotted fifteen minutes.

We sat in the room, facing the blackboard. I drew a line. On one end I put the word "triggers" with an arrow pointing to "response" at the other end. I then made a large curved arrow going from "response" to the space in front of "triggers." It was that simple. The answer was to go back to the beginning, realize what the triggers were and plant a different response in my mind. It worked for me. My yelling was decreasing even though my frustration was not.

By the end of my allotted time part of my mission took form: make the world a better place to live for my children. I was an untrained healer in the traditional sense; the university of life was my course—my unseen friends, my guardian angels, the guides. To change my world, I had to actively change myself. It was awesome. I became my own healer. Teaching others helped me clarify my thoughts, made me consciously aware of life and the abundance that exists.

My inner well-being and self-love manifested themselves. The treasure chest of positive affirmations opened with greater frequency, flooding my awareness.

The Hypnotherapist, the Psychiatrist and the Monkey on My Back (Continued)

One day I asked my hypnotherapist, "Did you give me a tape years ago with a woman's voice on it, telling me all was well in my world?"

"No," he said. "I only use my tapes."

My search for answers had begun in earnest.

Dr. Granite and I started setting the appointments further apart. I was finally ready to get off the lithium. Long-term use could damage my body. The fear my mother and my wife had was their problem, not mine. Toward the end of the year I started decreasing my use of the drug. This time I would rid myself of the psychological crutch other people assumed I needed. I would walk strong without it before they knew it was gone.

Massage was one way I dealt with my mind and body. It reaffirmed my self-love. Fortunately, I was introduced to a loving and caring masseuse who gave much more than I could ever repay. Her spirit and soul shone brightly like a guiding light. It was interesting how quickly changes occurred as people and events conspired to help my healing. I had awakened to a universe filled with abundance.

Good News—Bad News (Continued)

"You have sleep apnea, probably caused by your excess weight," the doctor at the hospital sleep clinic told me. "Your breathing pattern indicates that you stop breathing three to four hundred times in an hour. That is why you do not feel rested."

"What should I do?" I asked.

"Get a good night's sleep and lose weight. I will make arrangements to equip you with a CPAP unit. The machine forces you to keep breathing by gently pushing air into your lungs. Then you will get a good night's sleep and be better able to cope with life."

I was relieved that drug intervention was not needed. The messages my body was giving me were warnings. I had reached a critical decision point and started making healthier choices. There were many alternatives to drugs, and ultimately the answers all came back to one thing. It was up to me.

This knowledge awakened a spirit of exploration. I continued to read about food, diet, drugs and alternative methods of healing.

The bad news was that I realized the antibiotics so freely prescribed for my coughs and colds were killing the good as well as the bad bacteria in my body. They were not healing my body. It was like using a tank to shoot a glass off a fence.

When I spoke to doctors about their quick-fix approach, I was told that people expected a prescription or they would go to another doctor. The medical profession's addiction to money and lack of directness reinforced this vicious cycle. Neither the patients, pharmacists nor doctors seemed to be taking responsibility for what was happening.

What surprised me more was that doctors have a minimal level of pharmacological knowledge; pharmacists have more extensive knowledge. So doctors and pharmacists have an incestuous relationship, with neither taking full responsibility for what happens to the patients, who pay a horrible price: the potential loss of their bodies' natural healing abilities.

One day I got a yeast infection in my throat caused by the breathing medication I took. I went to the doctor at a walk-in clinic. He told me that the breathing medication inhaler caused the problem, gave me a prescription and sent me away. Then I went to the pharmacist and asked him why he had not told me that I had to gargle after using my inhaler. He blamed the doctor. No one took responsibility for what the drugs were doing to me, so I had to.

The heartburn and breathing medications had to go. I realized that alternative health choices existed, and the easiest one was to change my lifestyle. I stopped taking the drugs one by one. My mind felt like a sponge as I absorbed more and more information about aromatherapy, chiropractic, and anthroposophical medicine. This last is practiced by medical practitioners who combine herbalism and homeopathy with counseling. They believe healing is enhanced by acknowledging the connection between the mind, body and soul. The choices multiplied daily.

Food no longer replaced physical and emotional satisfaction once I realized that food was "the medicine cabinet for life" and its healing properties became abundantly clear. Herbs and spices took on a new role. They replaced the fat in my diet and stimulated my body to heal. Free of drugs, my mind regained its natural abilities to remember information and my past. I started feasting on life's physical abundance as I let go of one addictive pattern after another. I embarked on a journey with discoveries lurking at each turn. It was exhilarating.

My mind and body started slowly improving. I set time aside to walk two or three times a week and give myself the gift of solitude.

A friend had introduced me to the oldest healing profession on earth. Every few months, unknown to my wife, I went to see a lady of the night and just lay there naked beside her warm body as she caressed and held me. My tears mingled with the warmth of our bodies. It was the most sensuous of experiences.

I shared my thoughts and feelings with Dr. Granite. He rarely got a word in as I rambled on, pouring out my voluminous discoveries and new awareness. Something had to give. It seemed too good to be true.

I tried sharing my discoveries with those close to me. They had closed their minds to my pleas for them to think for themselves, especially when it came to their family's health. Who was I to tell people about such things, when I was a fat, smoking, ex-mental patient? They treated my messages with disdain. It appeared that the solutions I offered contradicted their expectations of the modern lifestyle and system of health care they were used to. It was a battle I could not win, but I could console myself with the fact that I had tried.

One after another, I saw problems occurring, with my children and those of friends and relatives, in ever increasing degrees. Asthma, learning disabilities, hyperactivity—the list grew, and with it grew my fear that our modern lifestyle was slowly killing our children's quality of life.

The more I probed and sought answers, the greater my distress became. Laini no longer would talk to me. Her fear and anger had taken control of her will to make conscious choices.

"Stop!" I pleaded. "Stop this insanity." Was I the only one who saw what was happening? No!

Vegetarianism, reflexology, "the healing hands of light." I felt guided by an unseen hand as I explored the inner world of thinking for myself, and experienced the wonders of a world of abundance. I discovered that all knowledge exists; our inability to uncover and accept it into our lives is what causes ignorance and fear.

I was on the path, but thirsting for a complete answer.

Chapter 11
A Sense of Purpose—1992

The year 1992 began peacefully. Laini and I took a trip to a ski lodge in the beautiful Laurentians. She skied, and I rested, walked and massaged my mind. I thought about the chaos I was living in: economic shambles and selling real estate which did not fulfil me.

That past fall, I had changed the asset mix of our retirement funds. Asset allocation was something I had intuitively been doing for two decades. I became aware of my perceptions of risk versus volatility in financial matters and how this related to my life. Risk is the chance of loss whereas volatility refers to fluctuations in the marketplace. In the short term, equities fluctuate a lot relative to supposedly safe investments like government-issued bonds. Over the long term, ten-year periods or more, equities have consistently higher returns. Confusing risk with volatility caused me to be reactive to situations rather than proactive. My old perceptions caused forceful actions and short-term thinking.

I could try to force events or learn to go with the flow. Life's ebb and flow seemed closer to the natural course of events. Everything began to make sense when I looked at and accepted the whole picture as being as it should be. My need to exert force was diminished.

With this understanding, I took a daring step and substantially changed our investment portfolios. That January, my intuition started proving to be correct. I had somehow connected to the universal force beyond my conscious awareness. I pursued my path of independent thinking. If I won, I was a hero; if I lost, I was a bum. Things beyond my control were at work, and I accepted this. My unseen friends guided me as I steered a clear course using a conservative back-to-basics approach. It worked with money as well as with most problems and events in my life.

Real estate sales took me out of the house. My motivation had switched to enlightened selfishness as I explored the world using my mind. That meant looking within before applying the knowledge to others.

My daughter Stephanie, then seven years old, was having difficulties in her social and family life as well as at school. Mixed signals confused Laini and me. Finally, the school tested her, and rated her as learning disabled. This meant she had measurable potential that exceeded her performance. Her daily frustrations and problems became ours.

Now we had a diagnosis and plan of attack. Laini and I started by giving our daughter drugs the doctors prescribed. I felt very uneasy about this. Their purpose appeared to be to control the child rather than helping her mind and body heal themselves naturally. The drugs were just Band-Aids, not solutions. I felt a need to get to the root cause of the problem.

Spring started, and Stephanie's light sleeping habits worsened. Laini and I had been aware of this since the night when she was a baby, when she had awakened and whimpered, and I had gone to cradle her until dawn. Sleep problems were causing Stephanie a lot of frustration. Her mind was very active. I searched for gentle ways to deal with the problem. Usually around midnight, Stephanie and I went for a walk. We talked about life. For a seven-year-old, that mean counting stars and smelling apple blossoms.

One night as we walked, Stephanie stopped, stared at the sky and said, "Star bright, star light, first star I . . . " Her voice trailed off as she squeezed her eyes closed. I looked at the stars through her eyes and realized they were God's tears of joy. I then reworded the wish-upon-a-star theme and said, "Stephanie, I believe it's meant to go like this: Starssss bright, starssss light, I wish all my dreams come true this night." At first she rebelled against the change, so I said her wishes and dreams were only limited by the number of stars in the night sky. It felt like a more complete and satisfying version.

Our walk ended, and we topped it off with a warm fruit drink at home. She easily fell asleep that night. I began to wonder what role the drugs played in her sleeping problems.

Our concern about the long-term effects of the drugs she was on were well-founded. The pharmacology book I consulted indicated possibilities such as sleeplessness, growth inhibition, addiction and to top it off, the possibility of a reduced life span.

"How had they found these things out?" I wondered. Then I realized that Stephanie was a living lab experiment, just as I had been. It made no sense to risk this precious child's life any further.

My zeal for replacing traditional drug therapies with alternatives accelerated when I read that there was a higher incidence of cancer in people using a drug I had taken for years. The price of the quick-fix drug approach was too high for me to accept. We stopped giving Stephanie medication and rationalized that we were getting her ready for her summer visit to her grandparents.

I realized drugs were being applied too often, and the drug makers did nothing to deal with this abuse. It fed their insatiable appetite for money to develop new and improved drugs to make more money. A reason underlying this is the fundamental principle that naturally occurring substances, without modification, could not be protected by the laws of man, so a subterfuge of sorts had been created by these mammoth money machines and by society at large. The illusion was created that healing best occurs with outside intervention. The fact that the body is a natural healing organism is overlooked. People are made to think that if it looks like a pill, you can trust it—an idea ingrained in me by the vitamin pills I took during my childhood. The rituals of dependency on others to do your thinking for you had fit in nicely with Western society's quick-fix mentality. It just did not seem to be working properly anymore.

Meanwhile, I discovered gold in my basement and shared it with my kids. Stephanie's sleeping problems were reduced by using the hundreds of record albums I had amassed. They became her treasure chest. She started listening to symphonies, instrumentals and the soft music from my collection. I remember one night helping her listen to dozens of classical records until she found just the right one.

"Why that symphony?" I asked her.

"It goes with the story in my head," she said.

The music therapy and the no-drugs approach appeared to ease Stephanie's sleeping problem. It helped her to understand the nature of her problem in an open and candid fashion with no stigma attached. More important, Laini and I had to deal with the feelings of guilt the educational system and our upbringing had forced upon us. In addition to these guilt feelings, our new course of action for Stephanie's care—and our marital problems—caused stress.

I embarked on a mission to help Laini and the kids understand that food could hurt or help them. There was more to food than just eating it. I pointed out that chocolate bars were a fat- and caffeine-loaded snack food, full of sugar. Stephanie realized she could make conscious choices.

I tried many ways, but the one that worked best was to give her choices. Going to the candy store was a learning experience. Helping Stephanie choose the best from a bad set of choices was an exercise in giving her back control over her life. I decided to guide her decision-making methods by only paying for candy made mainly with sugar, the better of the bad choices. Her allowance was big enough that she could pay for chocolate bars or fried potato chips herself. Stephanie was shrewd enough to know a good deal when she had one. It worked.

Months later, Stephanie and I were in a store. I no longer paid for any candy, preferring that she use her own funds. It let her take direct responsibility for her actions. I heard her saying to herself, "The chocolates have fats and caffeine, these are sugar only." The sugar candies are what she bought. This back-to-basics method of recognizing that the less junk in something, the better it was for her, worked.

At age seven, Stephanie understood that food had hidden effects, some good and some bad.

Laini became upset when I accepted her offer, one that she had made in anger, to take over the food shopping and menu planning. Laini's loss of control over these things put more strain on our marriage. I welcomed the chance to put my lifestyle and eating plan for the family into place.

The rule was simple: "Reduce the fat, cut out the crap." I started reorganizing the kitchen. Chips were replaced with pretzels and other crispy baked snacks. I stopped buying cardboard boxes full of highly processed foods. "Back to basics," was my motto.

The kitchen became a living classroom. Fruits, vegetables, whole-grain breads and seasonings became easier choices. I put the processed junk in the farthest corners of the cupboards, making them less accessible. At first, Laini and the children rebelled.

The signs of marriage breakdown were evident. Laini felt she could not talk to me and had chosen to get chocolate bars for her and the kids and hide them in her car, yet there was a board in the kitchen on which anyone could write their needs or wants. I filled everyone's orders on my shopping trips.

Our daughter's health care was being challenged by two widely diverse approaches and our adult egos. Neither one was necessarily the only choice, yet conflicts between them represented a fertile foundation for marital discord. My approach was becoming more a philosophy of life than just a way of eating. My belief in the spiritual world seemed clearer the more I got back to natural eating, healing and play. My mind and body became living proof of that as I began to feel and look better.

My spirituality was beginning to manifest itself slowly. I had taken back control of my life and my world. It made breaking the dependencies built up over the last decade due to my accident much easier.

Change is frightening to others who perceive it as a challenge to their world. The man-made world is imposed upon nature, creating its own form of chaos. My reality said that humanity and the universe were made to order. The natural abundance that the universal intelligence, God, had created was ours to share. The key was to give back more than you took.

The rate at which I was absorbing information was astounding. My mind, freed of the shackles of drugs and a poor lifestyle, sucked up the knowledge. It was not possible to impart to others all I was learning. I gave prerecorded audiotapes to others who did not have the time to read the books I had researched. This might seem a sign of mania, but I learned that other people who had followed the same path had experienced the same periods of leap-frog personal growth. My goal was not to reinvent the wheel, just to use it more wisely. I made conscious choices such as not watching TV, and choosing to read or go for a walk and think. I realized that many of the distractions of modern life were messing up people's minds and people hungered for easy answers and distractions, as if seeking refuge from the world around them.

Laini's fears and my rapid growth were reflected in our dissolving relationship. Changes to the nature of her business and the new direction of her career consumed a lot of her time. Going to numerous social agencies, tutoring Stephanie and seeking health and educational services to help Stephanie were demanding and draining for both of us. Our relationship suffered.

The Psychiatrist, the Hypnotherapist and the Monkey on My Back (Continued)

I was off lithium and functioning well. The members of my family could not terrorize me into taking the drug. Dr. Granite monitored me no more than once a month. I had understood the universal law that you must confide in at least one other person and God. In my case, I was lucky; I had many confidants: the masseuse, the lady of the night and an expanding circle of friends who accepted me for myself. All of these friends were very helpful. Sheri was one of them.

I met her at the community health club. She had gone through a tough divorce. I shared with her the idea that people should hire themselves. The simplicity of this concept had rekindled her sense of empowerment. Here was someone who accepted what I shared without being blinded by the baggage of my past. For me, it reaffirmed that my discoveries had universal appeal.

I began to reach out in more gentle ways, discovering that those who were ready to receive, did so, and those who were not, did not.

The power of touch and hugs is so primal that even newborns who are not cuddled begin to wither and die. My mother had taken a volunteer job as a "cuddler" of premature newborns at a hospital. I realized that modern medicine was gradually changing. It too had discovered accountability, caused by the economic downturn and a trend that showed more people seeking alternative approaches. The signs were not lost on the traditional healing professionals as their pocketbooks discovered the pain the public was experiencing. Sometimes a crisis is needed before people are willing to change. It appears to be a change for the better.

My own crisis of not getting the hugs and needed physical contact for my spiritual growth actually helped me become aware of how important touch is to inner peace and tranquillity. My crisis had become a good thing for my inner growth.

The lack of lovemaking meant that I did not feel guilty about seeking the comforts of the oldest healing profession. At every opportunity, I consciously turned a negative into a positive. No longer would I beat up on myself by denying my need for touch.

My relationship with the lady of the night was perfect. I paid my money and got held for as long as I wanted—that is, as long as it was not over an hour. It was a relationship with clear rules and boundaries. My need to protect my health and the health of those around me was safely dealt with this way. I did not want an emotional sexual relationship, as it would only confuse matters.

I believe psychiatrists and the whole mental health field could learn from this, and I hope they incorporate healing touch and hugging into their work. The power of human contact helps heal.

I was on the right "drugs," at last. I had found the magical healing formula. It was in my kitchen. Food. That, combined with walking, nature's most gentle and natural exercise, had wonderful effects. I felt healthier and happier.

My focus had shifted from weight loss to lifestyle management. This led to more gradual weight loss which my body could handle. My memory improved, and my thinking started to become more focused. The pain in my arm and shoulder eased somewhat. Even in this, I felt an unseen presence guiding me.

Good News—Bad News (Continued)

The realization that the drugs had effects far beyond what they had been prescribed for was good. It helped me intensify my search for alternatives. Unfortunately, this intensity was taken as a sign of mania by close family members. Fear had so clouded their thinking that they no longer dealt with me as an individual who had overcome adversities but as someone to be feared and avoided.

The more I took responsibility for my thoughts, actions and their consequences, the greater the subconscious resistance by those who resisted enlightenment. In May, I started asking questions about the school lunch program. It seemed odd to me that the school taught health and nutrition, yet missed the opportunity to show the children what healthier choices were.

It was evident that people did not directly deal with their problems, preferring instead to blame others for what happened. Educators'—in particular the bureaucrats'—lack of direct accountability in their educational guidelines and plans was a prime example. They pointed fingers at government funding and parents' demands. They paid lip service to requests for action if it meant change. Economically, most taxpayers were being destroyed by the recession. The majority of public school bureaucrats and staff lived a life relatively free of the economic stress and strains with which the general public lived.

In addition to this, many educators enjoyed long vacations and breaks during the year. This high degree of comfort, combined with lack of accountability, created a defensiveness on their part and bred complacency that obstructed their focus, which should always be the children. They feared that change could disrupt their domain and even destroy their security. Their addictive relationship to power and big paychecks and substantial benefits overcame their public mission of educating children.

Parents are just as responsible for this state of affairs. Their fear of change was evident in the way they initially dealt with my suggestions. Something had to give. The bad news is that I realized it was our children who were paying the price. How badly they were paying was becoming evident to me with my children and most educators' desire to keep the status quo. The economic crisis became their reason for cutbacks. This was evident in their resistance to test Stephanie as I had requested of her teacher the year before. In a sense, the bureaucratic mentality tied the teacher's hands.

Stephanie's reading problems had gotten worse over the year. The school had a policy of whole word reading, but it was okay for a teacher to use other methods to benefit their students. The whole word approach is when children learn words as whole units. Then the children break the words down into parts and learn how to make them into new words.

There was one problem with this. The school system did not supply the teachers with significant amounts, if any, of the needed tools, such as phonics reading primers. Again, the economy was the scapegoat. Unfortunately, parents have to pay in other ways. Laini and I paid by spending time, money and energy seeking help outside the system we counted on and paid to teach our children.

Laini made a commitment to be on the parents' liaison committee. I preferred to tackle the problem head-on, and directly approached the school board as well as the school itself. Laini's and my differing styles of tackling problems further worsened our relationship.

The extent of educators' and parents' resistance seemed to strike at the heart of our reason for being. People seemed to lack the combination of personal mission statements and goals for creating a dynamic, accountable educational system. The facades and lip service of an education system gone awry and parents' confusing quick fixes for solutions were destroying our children.

These insights started coming to me faster and faster. Something greater than I was guiding my education. The university of life had opened its doors, and I feasted on the abundance it provided. My intensity was not focused enough. I paid a price for this enlightenment: rejection by those around me. How could I deal with it positively?

The answer was the one I had come up with earlier in my voyage to enlightenment: If I wanted to change the world, I had to change myself. I had been doing this over the years as I came to terms with my trials and tribulations; now I could put it into practice, for my children.

My body signaled the correctness of this decision by tingling, something that happened more and more frequently. I accepted these positive life-affirming signals. The tingles, insights and intuitions I began to accept as gifts from God, a universal intelligence, not a tool to be used by other individuals to control the lives of people. Many traditional Western religions used man-made interpretations of the universal intelligence's messages of love, harmony and beauty to impose control and power over people.

The clarity of my thoughts and life took on a richness of their own. I was connecting to the world of abundance. Whenever I had a problem, I would ask myself: What now? This forced me to go forward in my thinking, rather then dwell on the past.

I remember suddenly having a need to call my mother. "You and Dad moved out of his mother's home when he was 44 and I was 16, right?" I asked her.

"Yes," she answered.

"Daddy never paid rent?" I asked.

"You're right," she said.

"I came from a poor family . . . " The insight flabbergasted me because 40 years of life had passed before I realized it. My dad loved to gamble, so we had been poor in the sense of money, but rich in the sense of love at home. This was hidden from me by my father's generosity. He would give a beggar his last dime if he thought it would help. This truth was the foundation of my scarcity mentality, which manifested itself by my need to acquire things. It was a hell of an awakening.

I began to understand why the famed therapist, Carl Jung, preferred to deal with those over 40. Generally, they were the people who dealt with crisis in life by seeking their spirituality. My mission became clearer: to help my children. It was my methods and need to set the mission on paper that I worked on.

The Ultimate Power

The good news was that I was making progress as I formulated a plan. The year had been my year of awakening, and the blossoming continued into 1993.

Chapter 12

The Trials by Fire—1993

Perseverance was the key. In her struggles my daughter exhibited a tenacity I admired. Her frustrations came out as anger, which was caused by the need of those around her to exert control. I was as responsible for this as they were, so I decided to use the ideals of Mahatma Gandhi and embraced and modified them to enhance my purpose for being.

I reasoned that passive civil disobedience by the masses began with one person—Gandhi. Obviously, I had to be willing to take the barbs that would be thrown my way. I started by consciously strengthening my inner harmony. I realized that my past and future were just figments of my imagination. How I perceived them was critical.

In January, I began a consistent program of walking. I had tried to exercise consistently for years, but had failed. My attempts were rigid. I would schedule three times a week to exercise and every time I missed a date, I would kick myself. Now I started telling myself to walk once a day, every day. If I missed a day I forgave myself.

My mind's power was the gateway to a bright future. I started unlocking the treasure chest of inner peace by walking and by massaging my mind. I discovered I was doing active meditation and it worked. It was one of the many techniques I used to help me focus within.

Another benefit of this lifestyle change was that the walking increased my stamina. My breathing had stabilized to the point where I used no drugs for my asthma. I lost weight slowly, and the sleep apnea stopped, so I finally got a good night's rest without the aid of the breathing machine. I felt great the day I retired the $3,500 machine to the closet.

My switch to healthier eating by reducing my fat intake had become a doorway to vegetarianism. I used simple tricks such as boosting the flavor of a food by adding more herbs and spices. They were part of the gift from the universal intelligence, a powerful gift to humanity that contained within it incredible healing properties. I discovered that over the long term, alternatives worked better for me than the traditional approaches.

I saw the Eastern and Western cultures beginning to work as one, each learning from the other, both trying to create a better world. It was no longer a matter of whose culture was best, but rather the realization that each had much to offer us. I was seeing life for the sensuous experience it was.

One day, the kids were having supper. Alan looked up and said, "Dad, are you a vegetable?"

"What do you mean?" I asked.

"At school they said you are what you eat, and you do not eat meat," Stephanie piped in.

I laughed. "I choose not to eat meat usually, but occasionally I do. But I am not a vegetable anymore. I am not a couch potato."

The dry humor was lost on them. Candidly, I think they are closer to the truth than I want to admit. I do accept the possibility that since humans are mainly made out of water, I could be called a bag of water in human form. That is why I refer to water as the wine of life. My children's attempt at labeling made me feel uncomfortable since the labels of my past had been used against me. It was something I realized people did to make their lives easier, not necessarily better.

I discovered the philosopher Friedrich Nietzsche had said it best, "To label me is to invalidate me."

The Psychiatrist, the Hypnotherapist and the Monkey on My Back—Conclusion

I stopped seeing the hypnotherapist at the beginning of the year. I had my focus and 1 did daily affirmations on my own. The sign of a true healer is that they can guide their patients onto a path of independence. The powers of self-love and self-discipline are awesome.

I made monthly visits to Dr. Granite, but the need had gone. I had been off lithium for a long time, with no signs of mania. That meant only people could stress me out, since my balanced lifestyle had built a better me.

In the spring, I started writing again. I wrote short-story observations about life. I saw my children and everyday folks as real heroes in the struggle to survive and thrive.

A friend asked me to write and send him an article about aromatherapy, since his dad had had a stroke and stimulating the sense of smell was a possibility in helping him recover. He published this article in one of his newspapers.

Smell is a primal sense that instantly awakens the body in more ways than one. It has many healing properties. During plague time people carried posies of sweet-smelling flowers to hold over their nose and mouth as protection against the "noxious fume" of the disease. Cleopatra used perfume to attract men. In the last century, the curative properties of the distilled essence from plant life, called essential oils, started being rediscovered by our society.

Mid-September was a time of great focus in my life. One night Alan was eating a bagel at the supper table and some of the bagels seeds fell off it. He stuck the seeds on his finger, looked at them, then at me and said, "Daddy, if I plant these seeds, will I grow a bagel tree?" That was the moment I learned how to do this simple miracle of growing bagel trees by using my imagination. That was when I wrote my signature story, "The Miracles I Have Seen: How to Grow a Bagel Tree." (You'll find story in Part II.)

The last time I saw my 47-year-old cousin Linda was in August, in the hospital. At that time, she shared her feelings and thoughts with me in more ways than I could ever express. That September, she died of cancer. I went to Montreal for her funeral.

I wrote a special epitaph for her, which I call "Linda's Song." (This story is also reproduced in Part II.) It is about life, death and becoming one with the universe. In truth, it is my epitaph. It is my belief that we are a part of the universal intelligence.

Writing can be a sign of mania. I believe mania in some cases is due to a creativity gene that enables humanity to rise to new heights. The danger is that the natural mechanism can break down and cause people to get out of control. Genetic manipulation is a two-sided sword. The excitement over genetic changes to life forms is due to the possibility of great profits. Natural substances cannot be patented. This legal, man-made right gives the drug companies a monopoly and they can price their drugs accordingly.

I fear some may wish to eradicate some perceived genetic defects for the sake of conformity, without fully understanding the long-term consequences. This need to control and pasteurize human beings into forced genetic conformity could sound the death knell for our species. History has taught us that, but have we learned the lesson?

On Wednesday, October 13, I gave Dr. Granite a copy of some stories and the book I had written as my legacy for my children. That Thursday, I faced a trial by fire. My family thought I was manic. Again.

They reasoned that I was obsessing about food, healthy alternatives and writing about the gifts of miracles in our daily lives. Their fear could have pushed me over the edge if I had not trained myself over the years to deal with it and answer them with love.

Again, the unseen hand intervened. The writings I gave Dr. Granite the day before were part of the materials he used to tell them that I had changed, that there were no indications of mania. People's fear of change is constant, rooted in their insecurities. In fact, the only constant is change and growth.

The power of the mind to deceive itself cannot be underestimated. It was the power of my mind that had enabled me to heal myself. Ultimately, it is one of the greatest strengths of humanity, a source of the ultimate power.

That October was the last time I saw Dr. Granite. All good things come to an end; his goal of helping me help myself had been realized. I had lived through this trial by fire with the grace and dignity of one who is on the right course—the path to unlimited potential.

The lady of the night and I parted ways; I no longer needed our monthly visits.

I had learned to live in awe. The universal intelligence and I had connected, finally.

My trials, tribulations and pains of the past became fertilizer for my mind, body and soul. They helped me learn to live in the moment and build a better me.

Chapter 13

Just a New Beginning— Now

The good news was that I lived through the past 11-plus years of trials and tribulations. In September 1993, a friend introduced me to a wonderful group called Toastmasters International. It is an international nonprofit speaking organization dedicated to helping people help themselves learn to speak in public.

On my first visit, a guest who had written articles for magazines, including *Reader's Digest*, told me that the group and I were in for a real treat. At that time, I did not know what she meant. Today I do. You see, that was the day I first shared my mission in life publicly. My guardian angels said it was time, and here it is: "I vow, each and every day to share with you the miracles I have found in this greatest of gifts called life. My mission is not to change the world but to fine-tune it for my children, all children." It is not the noblest of missions, just my reason for being.

It took me 41 years of living to discover that life is a gift, a treasure to be nurtured so that you and I may continue to grow and make this a better universe.

> *I am, as you are, a citizen of no land*
> *but a citizen of the universe.*
>
> —Ken Vegotsky

Part II

How to Unlock Your Mind-Body-Soul Potential

Chapter 14

How to Use the Keys to Unlocking Your Ultimate Power

The keys expand on the ideas expressed in my story; they are gateways to inner growth and self-discovery. Do you need a near-death experience to learn these keys to unlocking your potential? No! Not at all! My story gave you enough of a foundation of logic and emotion to accept these valuable life-enhancing keys. You do not need to experience the hell and traumas I did to become the person you want to be!

People learn best by example and practice, and this is the easy way to learn the keys. First, browse through the keys to get a feel for the messages I am sharing with you. Think of it as a leisurely stroll. Think of the keys as bricks; each one helps build a better foundation for your life.

Each key section consists of three parts.

Part 1 explains the key.

Part 2 gives examples of how the key applies to life. This is the emotional component of your learning process that helps you relate to the key.

Part 3 uses exercises and/or affirmations to show how to use the key.

Use this section as a reference source. Take time to explore the keys that interest you. Find practical applications in your daily life for each one. Each individual's style of learning is different. This leisurely approach to learning takes into account the naturally occurring phenomena of your mind, body and soul being one. This process takes time to develop to its fullest. The growth of your mind-body-soul connection can be fostered by the tools shared here. Savor the process so that you may enjoy your rise to a higher level of self-fulfillment.

Once you become more aware and accept these keys into your life, they will enrich your life. They will guide you to the realization that your mind is a key to understanding your perceptions. Usually, it is thought that the mind, referring to the brain, is in your body. The truth is that your body is in your mind—which is where the ultimate power resides.

All humans are spiritual beings, and realizing this is part of your journey. Intellectual awareness, combined with emotional acceptance and spiritual growth, will make your journey a highly rewarding and rich experience.

I have discovered that if you accept a truth fully, you have a greater possibility of more quickly becoming the fulfilled person you want to be. It is easy to say intellectually, "Killing is not right," but the test of whether you accept this idea would come during an emotional experience motivated by fear, such as being robbed or beaten. The way to get around that is to learn to deal with your fears and the fears others have by using the appropriate keys. Maybe you have to "Hire Yourself" or "Practice Forgiveness." The keys to these practices can be found in this section. In essence, the keys are forms of self-love. I define love as the spiritual heart of God, the universal intelligence. Your soul is God's reflection.

My purpose is to paint pictures that make you feel, so your mind and being can fully accept and absorb these thoughts and pictures. This is what the mind-body-soul connection is about.

Savor the ideas, and review them. Think of them as nuggets of gold that you are storing away until you need them. Gold has no value to a starving person on a desert island until that person is rescued. Plant these seeds in your imagination as you would in the earth. Cultivate them slowly with tender, loving care, and they will grow and blossom within you.

Your mind is a treasure chest where these thoughts will await your discovery when you need them. You will awaken to a life of con-. scious choices as you learn to live in awe of the moment.

How to Use the Keys to Unlocking Your Ultimate Power

"The journey of a thousand miles begins with the first step."
—Confucius

Congratulations! Your journey has begun.

Chapter 15

Hire Yourself!

You're fired! You're bankrupt! What do you do? Panic? Call for help? That's one possibility. But why not look for a new boss? Someone who is going to be there 100 percent of the time. Someone who believes in you. Someone who will kick you where you need to be kicked! Get the idea? Hire yourself!

During my recovery from the parasailing accident, I started making the greatest strides once I took responsibility for my well-being into my own hands. Then I began to feel in control of my life and my pain. The medical profession changed from being the master of my destiny to centers of information guiding my well-being. I drew upon their expertise and began to make my own decisions as to what would work best for me.

Problems still do arise, however, when people realize you've accepted full responsibility for what happens to you. I remember the nurses being upset when I decided I would allow them to take blood only once a day. It did not seem logical to me or my newfound boss to let them needlessly cause me pain when a little bit of coordination of their efforts, mixed with a dash of compassion, could enable them to do routine blood work from blood taken at one time. Once I made my wants clearly known, I was accommodated. Once a day it was, and once a day it stayed!

One day on our way to Stephanie's regular dental checkup, she commented, "Daddy, I like Ron. He fixes my teeth and takes care of them for me."

I was inclined to agree with her assessment of the situation, but this time I remembered my rule. When it comes to your well-being, hire yourself! With this in mind, I came up with a two-pronged approach.

Step one:

I told Stephanie that for her next visit to the dentist, she had a budget of $10 toward cleaning her teeth. I explained that if she did not need to have her teeth cleaned because she had done a good job brushing and taking care of them between visits, she could buy a toy with the money.

Step two:

I explained to the dentist my game plan. His role was to show Stephanie during that visit what her teeth looked like. His hygienist took the plaque that had been scraped off and showed it to her. They explained that brushing, flossing and rinsing would keep her teeth clean. Eating good things such as fruits and vegetables would help her build stronger teeth. The process became one of empowering Stephanie.

When I paid the bill, I let Stephanie know how much it cost and showed her with lots of $1 bills. I reminded her that next time she would have $10 and it was up to her if she spent it on the dentist or a toy.

Guess what? The next time, the dentist did not have to clean very many of her teeth, and he charged a reduced amount. Stephanie bought herself a doll. She had hired herself at the age of seven. Empowering children to be their own bosses is a great way to help them grow as people. Children start out empowered, but our society fosters the need for adults to control children. Relinquishing control and opting for the tool of guidance is a healthier choice for all concerned.

Take every occasion you can to practice hiring yourself and helping others to hire themselves. The more you do it, the easier it becomes. Use the three golden rules of learning: practice doing, practice doing and practice doing! It works!

Exercise:

This key to the ultimate power, like all the others, can unlock many doors for you. Try this exercise in hiring yourself: The next time you want to watch television, decide what kind of program you would like to see before you turn the tube on. Take a moment to consider what programs meet your

expectations. Then choose one. It is as easy as that to make conscious choices that benefit you the most.
Hire yourself!

Affirmations—repeat these frequently to yourself throughout the day:

- *"I am my own best friend. I hired myself."*
- *"I am making conscious choices in my life each and every moment."*
- *"I am loved and love myself."*

Chapter 16

Create Your Own Mission Statement

Discovering your reason for being, your purpose during this existence, gives you control over your life. It is a dynamic, ongoing process that keeps evolving as you grow.

My mission statement began as a feeling. Then it grew into a sense of purpose about improving the quality of my life. In my case, it meant dealing with my pain so I could do the things I wanted to in life. From the beginning of this dynamic process, I asked myself: "What is my purpose for being?" Slowly my mission dawned on me:

"I promise each and every day to share with you the miracles I have found in this greatest of gifts called life. My mission is not to change the world but to fine-tune it for my children. All children."

It is not the noblest of missions, just my reason for being. It is my mission during the human experience part of my spiritual existence.

To uncover my mission statement, I would write down my thoughts such as, "Life is a celebration" and review them, looking for a common thread. I discovered that the best way to change other people was to change myself. By deliberately causing inner growth through searching for a mission statement, my words and actions began to reinforce my life. Once I discovered that my mind, body and soul were connected, I understood that my mission must be holistically sound, or "user-friendly" to my universe and all those in it.

Exercise:

Summarize your life up to the present. Write your own obituary. Imagine reading it in the newspaper. If you do not like what you read, you can improve it. What would you like to read in your obituary? This exercise may seem macabre, so I will share with you the story about another person who used this approach. His name is Alfred Nobel.

Alfred's brother had died, and the newspapers accidentally put Alfred Nobel's obituary in their death notices. They remembered him as the inventor of dynamite, which had contributed to death and mayhem in the world. Alfred did not want to be remembered that way so he set out to create a mission statement that would fulfill his need to be remembered as someone who had added to people's lives. He wrote down his thoughts, and spoke to friends and acquaintances, sharing his ideas of what he wanted others to remember him for. His mission statement evolved, and gave him a new sense of purpose.

Today he is remembered worldwide as the man who helped recognize the achievements of those who add to the well-being of humanity. Decades after his death, Alfred Nobel is honored annually when the Nobel Prizes are awarded. His mission in life was accomplished.

Exercise:

Imagine yourself lying in a coffin. Look up and see those who know you. As objectively as possible, listen for their words and thoughts. It is their report card of your existence. These are some of the questions you might ask yourself as you fill in your report card:

Am I happy with what I heard? Did I become a better person in their eyes? Did I make the world a better place to live? Did I go far enough along the path to fulfilling my mission statement?

You are traveling according to your own compass setting and road map. You have to know where you are and where you want to go, if you want to get there with the least confusion and problems. Your mission statement is like a compass setting; it gives you direction. You consciously become the master of your life.

I have done many things in my life that I choose not to repeat as I learn from my errors.

Whenever in doubt, I remember that wonderful gentleman, Alfred Nobel, and his gift to humanity. Maybe it was no coincidence that his name and mission were so noble.

Affirmations—repeat these frequently to yourself throughout the day:

- *"I have a purpose and mission in life."*
- *"I am the master of my destiny, and my mission is my guide."*
- *"My mission in life is . . . "* *Fill in the rest yourself.*

Chapter 17

Use Your Goals
to Reinforce Your Mission

Goal setting is the ability to make your dreams and wishes come true. Goals may be short- or long-term objectives. For some people, their goal is to be wealthy; for others it is to attain happiness or raise a family. Positive goals that are life-affirming and environmentally friendly to those around you can reinforce or help in the creation of your mission statement.

Your goals are a way of building upon or making your mission statement a reality. They help fulfill your mission in life. As you achieve your goals, they help you live a life of conscious choices and joy, knowing you are headed in the direction you have chosen.

My first goal after the accident was to deal with my chronic pain and enhance the quality of my life. I used food to replace the pleasures in my life. In the process, I put on 90 pounds. It took me nine years to accept pain into my life as a friend that nurtured me. Only then did I start working on changing other aspects of my lifestyle. For example, I started to learn about nutrition, exercise and my mental abilities. These were bite-size aspects of my life that I started to change slowly. As I added the knowledge about each area of my mind-body-soul connection, I became more fulfilled. It was with this new awareness that I fully uncovered my purpose for being. The key was to use my goals, some stretching over many years, to help my mission statement evolve.

My son, Alan, loves people. His determination to make new friends at every opportunity is something he has consciously done since he was a toddler. One day he was riding his bicycle as I walked behind him. We came to an intersection. He said, "Daddy, I know all the kids who live in that direction, so let's go the other way and make some new friends." We did and sure enough, he made new friends. He was five years old at the time and had started to define his own goals. His sense of satisfaction and achievement is something I admire in him as he explores the world.

My daughter, Stephanie, was labeled a learning-disabled child at an early age. One day her teacher called in Laini and me to discuss various areas of weakness in Stephanie's education. At that point in my young daughter's life, her classmates could all count to 100, but she could not. We devised a plan. Stephanie was getting an allowance each week and obviously would appreciate a larger one. An arrangement was made whereby she could increase her allowance up to the point she counted to without making any mistakes.

Each Friday Stephanie sat with her mother and started counting before getting her allowance. Very little additional help was given, except practice counting the numbers beyond the point where she got stuck. Stephanie's allowance was 50 cents in the beginning. By the end of seven Fridays, her allowance had to be capped at 200 cents or we would have gone broke! Now she considers herself a mathematician as well as many other things. Go figure. We did, and she sure did!

> **Exercise:**
>
> Take a specific dream or wish you have that is positive. Make a picture in your mind of a specific positive outcome that motivates you. Make it attainable and realistic. By this, I mean bite-size. For example, you eat a whole watermelon, one bite at a time. Track your progress as you head toward your goal. You will be surprised by how quickly you get there.

Affirmations—repeat these frequently to yourself throughout the day:

- *"I am setting goals and making good choices each and every moment."*
- *"My goals add value to my life."*
- *"I love setting goals."*

Chapter 18

Imagination—How to Grow a Bagel Tree

Imagination is the key to unlocking your creativity. Use your life experiences as the basis for unleashing the creativity within you. Be resourceful and create new ideas using the fertilizer of your past experiences as building blocks. Use your imagination and recognize you have unlimited potential!

Alan was five years old when he created bagel trees. I had never heard of bagel trees before, but there he was, eating a bagel and looking at the seeds, when he asked me if they could grow bagel trees. His imagination spurred mine to create my signature speech story. What follows is a portion of this speech, first given to the New Horizons Toastmasters International club in fall 1993.

The Miracles I Have Seen: How to Grow a Bagel Tree

Someday I'll write the stories of the big miracles I have seen, from the man on the moon, and the fall of the Berlin wall to the signing of the Middle East peace accord in the President's garden of roses. Wistfully I say, "Maybe one day I'll write them." Until then, I content myself with the small miracles that abound daily.

I wake up in the morning and this start of the new day is miraculous enough for me. At night I crawl my weary bones and tired body into bed beside that other simple miracle of daily life, my wife of 16 years. That too is wondrous enough for me.

You see, it is the simple miracles of daily life that wrap me in wonder. That is what life is about.

Now, take Alan, my 5-year-old pride and joy, who is going on 30. He is a miracle that brightens my every day. Last night he did it again!

I had bought some fresh bagels, those round doughy things with a hole in the middle. They were covered in little white sesame seeds that always seem to seek and find the gaps between my teeth.

Anyway, here was Alan holding this circle of delightful dough in his tiny hands, happily munching on his bagel. Suddenly, he stopped to ask me, "Daddy, if I plant these seeds, will a bagel tree grow?"

A close friend started to answer him in her typically linear way. I, being the foolish soul I am, took my life in my hands to interrupt her and say, "Alan, if you believe in bagel trees, let's plant the seeds and see."

Well, I don't know about you, but until today I did not believe in bagel trees. Just in case they might exist, Alan and I planted the seeds. You know what? I would not be surprised at all to see bagel trees grow . . .

In any case, I have proof enough to know that bagel trees really do exist in the imaginations of 5-year-old boys and 41-year-old dads.

Such are the wonders of childhood and parenthood, an awakened sense of discovery and the pleasure of living in the moment. Listen to children. They have much to teach you and me about the miracles of life and using our imaginations.

This is what imagination is all about. Using Alan's simple question and questioning myself about other experiences I had had helped me realize the events of daily life are miracle enough for me. Using your mind to combine your experiences and come up with new ideas is imagination in action.

History supplies us with abundant examples of imaginative people. Using their imaginations, the Wright brothers helped humanity take flight. Thomas Edison shed light on the night. These are examples of imagination in action. Where does it begin? In your mind.

Exercise:

Close your eyes and imagine yourself walking past a bakery. You smell freshly baked bread, chocolate cakes and sweet honey buns. The smells permeate the air and you inhale deeply. You start to salivate.

That is the power of imagination in action. It creates results!

Affirmations—repeat these frequently to yourself throughout the day:

- *"I use my imagination to improve myself."*
- *"My imagination is wonderful."*
- *"I imagine myself being the person I want to be."*

Chapter 19

The Magic of Creativity

Creativity brings into our reality ideas, inventions and an endless list of simple and grand things. When I wanted to give my nerve graft and transplant operation a greater chance for success, I asked the professionals at the rehabilitation center to see what they could come up with. Motivated by my challenge, they created a mechanism that let me put my arm in a movable sling so I could maximize my exercise efforts on my arm, at home.

Their creativity is what made the contraption possible so I could help myself more often.

Alan is a very creative child. He loves people. Whenever he meets other children, he tells them up front that he wants to be their friend. If he has a candy or toy, he offers to share it with them. He creates friendships.

Amelia Kunkle Devine was 16 when she joined the Salvation Army in 1900. Quickly she discovered that the busy people of New York did not give as much money to the needy as she had hoped they would. In 1902, she bought a small bell, stood on the street and rang it to attract donors. The amount she collected skyrocketed! Soon after, The Salvation Army started ringing bells around the country. Emma's desire to be a more effective fund-raiser helped bring food, shelter and clothing to millions. In her way, she helped fine-tune our world, and so can you with a dash of creativity!

Exercise:

On the next page is a small square. Take a pencil and do something with the square.

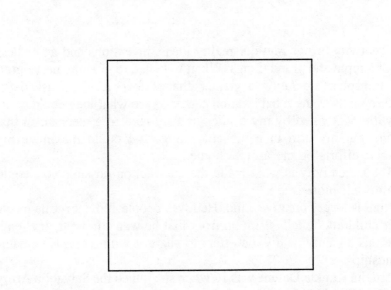

Please read after doing the preceding exercise.

Explanation:

When I did this with a group of adults, some filled in only the insides of the box, and others incorporated the box into a much larger picture. The page and box are like your life. Life is what you make of it. Be creative, and go beyond the bounds you have created for yourself. Creativity is imagining in action!

Affirmations—repeat these frequently to yourself throughout the day:

- *"I love to create."*
- *"I am fulfilled when I express my creativity."*
- *"I am a creative person rising to my level of self-fulfillment."*

Chapter 20

Practice Believing

Believing is an act of unconditional acceptance. It starts within yourself, and the world around you is the reflection of your beliefs. Believe you are a good person and that there is a universal intelligence you are part of. The more you practice believing in yourself and the reality of God, the fuller and richer your life will become.

Before my first major surgery, I was fearful and angry at the world and all those around me. Why had they let this happen to me? What had I done to be punished like this every moment of my existence? Only bad things happen to bad people, I thought. My mind had lost its faith in me and the universal intelligence, God. I was doomed to a living purgatory, hell on earth!

Then it happened, when my life was at its bleakest point, and I tried to reach out with pills, booze and distractions, begging for help. I had almost succeeded when I got the message again. It took many times before I finally bought into it, but that night as I lay in bed, my faith was restored. I had started to believe in myself and the universal intelligence again. It took many years of tests by fire until I at last accepted the truth that I am a citizen of no land, but I am a citizen of the universe, just as you are.

Years of painful struggles finally came to fruition through the magic of believing. Do you need such extreme pain to learn as I did that belief and faith are one and the same? No! Not at all! Seek and find the answers within yourself, and you will be fulfilled.

Stephanie was nine years old when her school was having a countrywide test of students in third grade, to assess the current state of our educational system. Her principal sent a letter and called us, recommending that Stephanie not take the test as it might be too stressful for a learning-disabled child. My wife and I believed in Stephanie and her right to fail as well as succeed. We saw in this opportunity a chance to help her feel a part of the whole and know that it is okay to fail, since her success was just that she tried.

Many weeks later, the results came back. The special education teacher and her classroom teacher were surprised at how well Stephanie had done. Their measurements were only a small part of the greater good this opportunity had created for my coparent and me to practice believing in our wondrous learning-disabled child. In our eyes, she had already succeeded!

Belief is the mirror of your soul. Some think it only the territory of religions, but it is not; it is a key to unlocking your potential as you practice believing in yourself and God, daily.

Exercise:

When you go to sleep tonight, write the following on a piece of paper and plant the thought in your mind, "I am drifting into a deep, restful sleep. I will awaken rested and refreshed."

Put the paper near your bed where you can read it first thing when you wake up.

This is the art of consciously believing in things you take for granted. Each and every day practice the art of believing as you go through your day. You turn on the tap and out comes water. You walk out of your room, and suddenly you are in the next room. In both cases, it is your beliefs that created these thoughts. Up to now, you took them for granted. Now you realize that all your life you have practiced believing in your physical world. Now it is time to extend that art of belief beyond your body and physical being into your mind and soul.

Exercise:

Sit or lie down in a comfortable, safe place.

Close your eyes a moment and take a deep breath. Hold it a few seconds, slowly exhale and savor the passage of air into and out of your lungs and body. Let yourself relax.

Take another deep breath and savor the oxygen as it enters your brain, invigorating your mind.

Now take a third and final deep breath. Be relaxed. Believe in your ability to affect your world from within. Know your inner self is the source of all your beliefs.

Then, slowly, let your breathing come back to normal. You feel good and calm.

Restoring the power of belief within allows you to enhance your world and your potential.

Oxygen in the air is good for you. This is a belief you always held from the moment you were born, yet take for granted. Your focus on the outside world begins and ends in your mind and your beliefs.

Exercise:

It is the choices you make that show what your hidden beliefs are. They are a reflection of your being. This exercise reinforces your positive beliefs about yourself.

Mentally make a list of your good traits. I believe I am a caring and sensitive person who sees life as a sensuous experience. Use words such as, "I am intelligent . . . caring . . . loving . . . sensitive . . . wonderful." Choose whatever positive descriptions of yourself you can think of. Make the list as long as you want.

Then write down this list of thoughts about yourself. In this way, you see what is positive in you.

If your list is too short, write down those thoughts about yourself like this, "I am a loving person. I am a caring person." Keep looking at that paper many times in the following days, and you will discover that you are consciously becoming all those things you believe about yourself.

Affirmations—repeat these frequently to yourself throughout the day:

- *"I believe I have unlimited potential."*
- *"I believe that my mind, body and soul are in harmony and one with the universe."*
- *"I believe in me."*

Chapter 21

Conscious Choices
and Your Perceptions

Conscious choices are about being aware of the thoughts and ideas you are having about the world you live in. Your past, present and future are all unconsciously one. The happenings of your past are like an audiotape, unconsciously replaying themselves all day and night. Your past becomes the basis for how you deal with people and events. This is the hidden power of your mind, a reflection upon your world.

Learn to trust yourself by making a decision to turn your will, your life and care over to God, the universal intelligence. Seek freedom by not letting others think for you but by learning to live in the moment and find the awe in life. Live in perpetual awe and discover the sensuality of your human experience and your spiritual being.

In my addresses, I call myself a well-disguised Robert Redford, Christian Slater or Errol Flynn. On the outside, my rotund figure does not in any way look like any of these handsome men. My body is what most people perceive as me and their thinking stops there. I take them the next step and tell them the main difference.

"Robert Redford is richer and better known than I am, at least today," I say, pausing for a moment. "But on the inside, we are both alike: kind, good and caring people."

Conscious choice deals with your buried perceptions about yourself and your world. By using awareness, you are taking your inner eye—unspoken beliefs, rules and thoughts about life—and seeing them honestly for what they are. Then you can start to deal with them. The following story is an example that helps people understand that it is what is inside your mind, body and soul that matters most.

One day, Alan and I were at the park. I had a rule that if he was in the climbing play area, I would help him once and only once during that visit. My belief and perception was that if he got up to the top, he could get down if he perceived he could. This was my experience in life; if I mess up, I have to take care of my own mess.

I wanted him to learn that he had to live with the consequences of his choices, and this was the safest way I could do it. That also meant he would have to learn to deal with life's struggles as we all must ultimately do, by dealing with our inner selves. This has a lot to do with our perceptions. Alan climbed to the top of the climbing area with my help. Once he got there, he did not see himself coming down without my help. I sat listening to music on my Walkman as I heard him yelling for help.

The ground rules were set. I wanted to help him but this would have cheated him out of an opportunity to succeed. I find that I confuse guilt as love because of the way I was brought up. The guilt of my past welled up inside me as I waved back at him and pointed to the headphones on my portable cassette player, motioning that I could not hear him. I was not listening to music at that time, but he did not know that.

Ten minutes later, he walked up to me. He was upset and told me so. Then he went back to the climbing area. Over the next hour, he scampered to the top and back down, without my help.

Alan's perceptions created fear, and it was best answered with the love of a parent who knows you can create conscious choices and deal with your perceptions positively. Alan at the age of five learned one of life's most important lessons in a caring and safe situation. Sure, I would have helped him if his distress were based on the reality of his being hurt rather than in his perceptions of incurring for himself possible pain.

Conscious choice is the difference between having sex and making love. Sex in a scientific sense is purely an instinctive survival mechanism. Lovemaking is God's gift to you as you go farther along the path and become more connected to your spiritual being. Learning to share the energy and ecstasy of lovemaking requires that you be consciously aware of your partner's actions, reactions, feelings and experience before, during and after lovemaking. It is one time where your mind, body and soul meld into one totality.

To add zest to a long-term physical relationship with another person, I approach lovemaking with that person as a new experience each time. I consciously choose to believe that it is the first time I am sharing my mind, body and soul with that person. It may be the hundredth or thousandth time, but in my mind it is like the first time. This is a journey of exploration and discovery, one of learning to share and sharing to learn.

It is like playing the piano. Each time a pianist sits in front of the piano keys, the musician can choose to either hit the individual notes or to create a symphony. It still is just a piano, but when it comes to living consciously, I believe you have a choice whether you play notes or create your own symphony of life.

The French have a perfect description for the culmination of lovemaking. They call the orgasm "le petit mort," which means "the little death." It is one time when you completely lose control over your mind, body and soul. These three parts of your being become one with the universe for a brief moment in time. It is a brief and delirious moment that can only be compared to death, since it is such a vibrantly refreshing acknowledgment of your human experience.

Conscious choice means that your perception of your physical being, your body, is really in your mind. This is a key to attaining total spiritual satisfaction and becoming one with the universe.

Conscious choice lets you deal with mind, body and soul by taking responsibility for what happens to you. Learning to live in the moment is experiencing conscious choice as the universal intelligence planned.

Exercise *(Read the following and then do it)*:

You are looking at yourself in the mirror. What you see is someone else's body. (If need be, use your imagination for the next step. That is how I saw myself as a well-disguised Robert Redford. No snickering, please.) See in front of you the body of the most sensual and desirable person you can imagine. Look at the magnificence of this creation called a body. Be in awe of its miraculous healing properties, its awesome potential for experiencing life to the fullest. Savor the beauty of what you see.

Now say to yourself, "I am seeing God's greatest creation, my body and mind. God gave me a body, for the human experience part of my spiritual journey. God gave me a mind with which to explore my universe so I may go farther along the path of my spiritual existence. God gave me my soul so that I may live in conscious choices every moment of my existence. I choose to live in awe of life, my body, my mind and my soul."

Reread this whenever you feel the need to reaffirm your reason for being, or feel in pain during the physical part of your human experience. This will help you realize your body is in your mind and that you are indeed a miraculous creation.

Affirmations—repeat these frequently to yourself throughout the day:

- *"I am living in awe of life."*
- *"I am consciously living my sensual adventure called life."*
- *"My mind is the key to my perceptions."*

Chapter 22

Be Honest with Yourself

Accepting that "your body is in your mind" is one key to your perceptions. It allows you to free yourself from the projections of others about what is beautiful or good. Honesty is being truthful to yourself in a frank and open way. Using this honesty helps you deal with your self-perceptions.

Make a diligent soul-searching inventory of who you are. Realize that what you see in others is but a reflection of your own beliefs and perceptions.

What I see on the outside is not what I know is on the inside. No, I am not Robert Redford, nor do I want to be him or anyone else, for that matter. I am a middle-aged, partially paralyzed man with a rotund physique. I am living separate from my wife as we head toward divorce. At times my hormones get the better of me. Sometimes I get upset and yell, but most times I choose not to.

On the inside, I see myself as someone who has found inner peace and solitude. I see life as a sensuous adventure in a body constantly in pain in the traditional sense, yet I see my pain as my medium for growth. I have a wealth of experience, and choose to use my past as the foundation for a renewed me, each and every day. I am honest with myself and ask those around me to be honest with me, too. The danger with honesty is that you can use it as a reason not to go beyond your perceived limitations. That is also the side of honesty that is most powerful. My honesty with myself is a key to my growth and fulfillment. It is your key also.

"Ken, you're a pain in the butt," I sometimes hear myself say, and it is true! When I feel committed about something, I believe I must take positive action. Here is a case in point:

The school my children go to provides a pizza lunch with a snack every two weeks. When I discovered that fat-laden potato chips was the snack, I went about trying to get the school to change it. I felt it was inappropriate for a school which taught children about health to serve unhealthy food. I believe it is more important to show children than to just tell them what healthy eating is about.

I give the principal credit; he chose to discontinue serving chips as a snack, yet a majority of parents were upset by this change. Any attempts to use healthier choices such as apples or low-fat baked foods were met with considerable resistance. It got to the point where a demanding list of criteria for what the apples had to look like and how they had to be handled was drawn up. I'm sure that even the Garden of Eden did not have apples that perfect.

The bureaucrats were caught between parents who wanted their children to have healthier choices and those who wanted to maintain the status quo. I was disappointed that the children were prevented from having a rewarding and positively enriching experience.

I got and sent free course materials on fruits and vegetables to the school board. I also sent a simple proposal. I suggested in writing that they implement an "Eat Your Way To Health Day" each month. This would be an opportunity to show and tell the children what better food choices are about.

Our schools have an environmentally friendly approach of reducing, reusing and recycling. They even dedicate a day each month to reduce, reuse and recycle. It seemed logical to me that my proposal was sound and safe. The teachers in the school used and enjoyed the materials I sent, and so did the children. The bureaucrats on the school board ignored implementing the use of these high-quality professionally produced materials, even though they supplemented their educational programs. A year later, my children had a pizza lunch, but still no snack, still no "Eat Your Way To Health Day."

At the end of the year, I sent a letter to the chairman of the school board and the school. I answered their fear of controversy with love. I hope that by now educators and parents will have learned to be honest with themselves and understand that our role is to guide our children, not possess or just react to them. I hope they show their commitment by implementing a program of healthier snack choices and an "Eat Your Way To Health Day."

I am honest with my children and have shown them what healthier choices are about. My daughter, who was on medication for her learning disability, is no longer on drugs. Food is just one part of the answer—not the whole answer—yet it is one that my children were being made aware of at as early an age as four.

I saw my fear that my children would repeat the errors of my ways. What I discovered was the fear in others of change, their fear of being honest with themselves. The price they pay is the present and future quality of the lives of our children.

Honesty is something our daily news reports on. Not sensationalism alone, but the dishonesty in our system. Read about one politician after another who defrauds the public and undermines our trust in the democratic system. These people may rationalize their choices, but their lack of honesty hurts us all. Have you ever not paid a tax that you should have paid? It's easy to say everyone else isn't paying their full share, so why should I?

Fine, let's accept those ideas as truths for a moment. If taking every opportunity to evade taxes is the case, then what would happen if we all paid the taxes legally due? Is it possible your taxes would be lower? Is it possible fewer bureaucrats and law enforcement officers would be needed to find and recover the unpaid taxes? In my naivete, I choose to believe that society and our children would benefit with just a tad more honesty in taxation matters. The next time I get a chance to evade paying a sales tax, rather than do that, I will not. In this way, I give back to society a little of the values it has given me, by paying the tax. Will you?

Exercise:

Reread the preceding paragraph. When the opportunity comes, seize it and realize you are being honest with yourself by your actions and choosing not to cheat your society of money. Being honest in this way reaffirms your values and our society's worth.

Pat yourself on the back for being honest with yourself and not letting greed devalue your worth.

Exercise:

This is more fun. It will not cost you money. It will be of great value to you.

Imagine the most dishonest thing you have ever done. Smile. Remember how good it felt? Did you cheat someone? Lie to someone? Steal a million dollars? (Forget the last one, I know temptation has its limits.)

Now, imagine you are the person or individual in the group who suffered from this action. Feel the pain and frustration you suffered, as if it were your own.

Are you feeling guilty, bad, sad or mad about the feelings you caused others to have? Vow to yourself that when another similar opportunity presents itself, you will be honest. Acknowledge that you may want to do a negative thing but are making a conscious choice not to. Picture in your mind how good you feel by showing this restraint. Pat yourself on the back. You were honest with yourself and did not devalue your self-worth by deed or action.

Affirmation—repeat these frequently to yourself throughout the day:

- *"I am honest to myself."*
- *"I see myself for who I am and am becoming a better person for this."*
- *"I love and accept myself."*
- *"I see myself as others see me."*

Chapter 23

Be a Winner
in the Lottery of Life!

Winning the lottery of life meant that I had to let go of the negative aspects of the past. My anger had turned into depression, and my fears had become anxiety. I was letting my past destroy my present. I had to let go of the past to survive. It was a gamble I had to take.

The night I took pills and booze, trying to bury my past, I remembered the parasailing accident and my purpose in life. I decided to use my past to help me. In my pain I found a fertile medium for inner growth. I thought of it as "the garbage of my past had become the fertilizer for my present, helping me grow a better tomorrow." Thinking of it this way enabled me to start growing inside again.

Recently I went to the park with my children. They scurried all over the jungle gym. I sat and watched with satisfaction, as a year before Alan had been afraid to climb down from the top of the same piece of equipment. I had refused to help him, and said that if he got up the tree, I knew he could get down if he chose to. His displeasure with me then was both vocal and prolonged.

Here he was now, climbing and swinging like a monkey. Suddenly he stopped, scampered down the jungle gym and ran toward me. He said, "Daddy, remember last year when I tried to do this, how scared I was? It's easy. I love you." He triumphantly smiled, turned and rejoined his sister.

Although at the time, I'd been unsure if I'd done the right thing, the result I saw now was a happy, independent child. Alan had built upon his past anger and had realized it. I felt loved and proud.

The Ultimate Power

The Echo Newspaper in England in 1994 reported that the next Lord Mayor of Liverpool, age 53, had been found guilty of prostitution in the 1970s. In 1990, she'd been fined for "conspiring to obtain property by deception." The politicians of the city of Liverpool rallied around this woman. They understood that her past was a learning experience and she had become better for it.

Building on your past starts with yourself. That is how to become a winner in the lottery of life. A little help is appreciated, when needed.

> Exercise:
>
> Imagine yourself when you first began to ride a bicycle, play a sport or read. Were you upset, frustrated or angry during any of these activities? Are you still upset about the things that frustrated you then? No. That is how your past builds a new present and future for you.

Affirmations—repeat these frequently to yourself throughout the day:

- *"My past builds me a better today."*
- *"I accept what has passed and use it to make me strong now."*
- *"The poo-poo of my past is my fertilizer for today, which helps me build a better tomorrow."*
- *"I am a winner in the lottery of life."*

Chapter 24

Give up the Need
for Control

Control is a desire to exercise authority over yourself and the world around you. This desire and power to direct and regulate has broad-ranging applications, some good, some bad. The key to maximizing the benefits of control lies within you.

Giving up the unconscious need to exert control on the people, places and things around you can be very beneficial. Where does this need come from? How can you benefit from it?

Observe babies. Stephanie's and Alan's births were routine deliveries. They started life being separated from their mother. First, a doctor took them from the womb, a nurse cleaned them and then they were given back to their mother for a short while. Unfortunately, control was exerted on the babies and mother by the nurses who followed procedures and separated Stephanie and Alan from their mother. At the time, we were told this was so their mom could rest. Now I believe this is the beginning of the Western world's model of control that is exerted upon children. The effects of this control are felt throughout their lives.

As the children grew, I observed their need to make sense of their world. They did this by exerting control upon people, places and things. Stephanie and Alan would cry out for food and comfort. Their mom and I responded to their demands in a variety of ways. We were being controlled by what appeared to be their physical needs and wants.

As the children aged, their explorations were expressed in a seemingly innate desire to put things in their place. If changes to their man-made world occurred without the children's permission, they became upset. Exerting control was how they learned to strive, survive and thrive. Was it necessary? Is being in control the most beneficial way to deal with life?

I noticed that Stephanie, then Alan, seemed to exert their desire to control mainly upon the man-made objects and spaces in their lives. When they played in natural settings, this need was not as strong. They accepted the way the world of nature was and played in it, laughing, giggling, crawling, being explorers. Generally, they seemed happier in natural surroundings.

Again, we exerted control. When it rained, we put on the children's rainwear and boots. "Watch for puddles," we would say. "Stay away from the bushes! Don't go there!" Their innocence was lost by age six—their natural desires to explore and discover had been greatly curbed, by us. Unconsciously, we had duplicated the models our parents had thrust upon us. Did we really do this for their benefit? Or was it for ours? Is this the best model for survival? In some regards, for perceived purposes of safety, it seemed so. I have come to question this, however, based on my post-accident discoveries.

When I nearly died, I entered a state of inner peace and tranquillity that intervention from the outside world destroyed. I was not breathing when they fished me out of the water onto the dock. It was the need of the people on the dock to intervene and bring me back to life, something I knew would have occurred anyway, that caused much of the trials and tribulations I later suffered.

Mouth-to-mouth resuscitation, drugs, ambulances and an interventionist medical model turned my world upside down. I lost control over my life and my pain. My growth was stunted, not promoted. Once I no longer followed these external control models and took back control of my life did I start to heal more fully.

It took years of inner struggles to succeed. When I had my shoulder fusion and Steindler surgical procedures performed, my control was again violently taken away when the nurses injected me with morphine to kill the pain. Again, I lost control and was buried beneath a tide of pain. The Band-Aid of drugs prevented me from exercising my abilities to deal with pain, and heal. The task I had started working on earlier was pushed back many years.

Control can be an insidious form of external or self-imposed destruction when it is misapplied. A historical analogy is Hitler's attempt to take control of Russia. His armies marched thousands of miles, to the city of Stalingrad. The Russian army and citizenry put up a valiant defense. The long supply lines to maintain Hitler's army grew strained. His troops were worn down by the very need to control that led them to their many victories.

Somehow, the Russians, attacked by Hitler's armies, bravely stood their ground. What was it that enabled them to survive this horrific assault and resist the might of Hitler's army?

The answer is that they controlled their immediate world. Their self-love and self-discipline allowed them to survive the harsh Russian winter against insurmountable odds. Hitler's troops gave up their attempt at exerting control upon the world. Defeated, they retreated. The Russian Army and citizenry, by astutely managing to control themselves, had defeated one of the most powerful armies on the face of the earth at that time. They were able to prove that control within oneself is the greatest form of power one can exert upon the world.

Self-discipline is control you exert upon yourself. Self-control is not needing to physically force or manipulate another. It requires an inner strength and will. The more you practice it, the easier it becomes to allow others into your life—the easier it allows you to receive into your mind, body and soul the abundance the world has to offer.

Exercise:

Step 1

This requires two people to demonstrate the power of control. Find a partner of roughly equal strength, and a quiet place to sit, facing each other. Raise your right or left hand, flat palms touching your partner's hand. With all your might, both of you push against each other's hands, expending energy for a short while.

What happens? Neither of you gets anywhere. Your hands stay suspended in the same place. Eventually, your energy is drained, muscles are tired, and if you have invested emotional content into winning, you are frustrated. By exerting physical power, you got nowhere.

Step 2

Repeat the above exercise, but with one difference. Your partner exerts force, you use your hand to guide the direction of your partner's hand by offering no resistance. Where do you both end up?

Your hand and your partner's hand end up being closer to your body. Your partner exerted most of the effort and energy, you received them into your space. Your partner's arm could go no farther; it was stretched to the limit. You, on the other hand (pun intended), had relinquished external control, opting for self-control, and so you expended very little energy.

Your partner's hand ended up by your side. His or her energy was expended and yours was conserved. In essence, he or she became part of your sphere of influence. By relinquishing your need for external control, you gained mastery over yourself and your world.

Exercise:

Read and study the life of Mahatma Gandhi. His philosophy to promote change was one of passive civil disobedience.

Exercise:

Make time for yourself. Find a peaceful place, preferably in a natural setting, such as a forest. Stand, sit or comfortably adjust your body to the environment. With your eyes, explore the abundance around you. When ready, close your eyes and listen to the world of sounds and life surrounding you. Let your mind-body-soul receive life's abundance.

These exercises demonstrate that self-control heightens your senses, levels of stimulation and control over your life. Enjoy.

Affirmations—repeat these frequently to yourself throughout the day:

- *"I trust myself and those around me."*
- *"I believe in my abilities to control myself."*
- *"I no longer need to control others and prefer to receive freely the abundance my universe and God offer."*

Chapter 25

Practice Thankfulness

"How are you?" is a common question. Listen to what people say. You will be amazed at the list of complaints and negative attitudes you hear. Practicing thankfulness is about not taking life for granted. It is a talent you can rediscover. Each moment is a gift, which is why it is called the present! Becoming thankful is one way you show appreciation for this gift.

After my accident, I had trouble walking up a flight of stairs or 50 feet to the corner of our street. At first I used a cane, and was thankful for having one. I realized that time was my ally as I used time to allow my body to heal. I came to realize that I was lucky to have one working lung to get me through the day. All these small things began to add up to one big thought: I was thankful just to be alive.

Now when someone asks me, "How are you doing?" I answer, "Any way I can," or, "I got up this morning and that's enough for me." Thankfulness helps me not take life for granted, each and every day.

"Thanks, Daddy," are two of the most beautiful words a child can share with a parent. My children are learning to acknowledge the big and little things in life. Here is thankfulness in action: yesterday my daughter left a beautiful singing message on my answering machine.

Sung to the tune of Happy Birthday:

Verse 1

Happy love day to you
Happy love day to you

Happy love day to you
I love you loads too!!!

Chorus: Kiss . . . kiss . . . kiss . . . kiss

Verse 2

Happy hugs and kisses to you
Happy hugs and kisses to you
Happy hugs and kisses to you
I love you loads too!!!

Chorus: Kiss . . . kiss . . . kiss . . . kiss

Song created by Stephanie July 31, 1994. Received with thanks by Dad.

Exercise:

Get that singing voice in your head ready. You can practice silently at first. Now go to your mirror and belt it out as best you can.

"Happy love day to you . . . Happy love day to you . . . "

Great, I see you're getting into the spirit of thankfulness already. I look forward to the time you and I meet so we can all sing this song of thankfulness off-key. I have more where that came from, thanks to my children.

Affirmations—repeat these frequently to yourself throughout the day:

- *"I wake up and that is good enough for me."*
- *"I am thankful to be me."*
- *"My life is a gift from God. Thank you for my gift."*

Chapter 26

Welcome Crisis into Your Life

Crisis is a turning point at a crucial time or event. Usually it is seen as a bad thing. In fact, you can make it into a positive event. How you deal with crisis determines the outcome.

When my daughter was six years old, she was labeled as learning disabled.

This was definitely a crisis for her and her parents. What do we do? Where do we go? Is there an answer? In anger I lashed out at a school system, a system with a different set of priorities than mine, while I coped with my feelings and my learning-disabled child. Guilt and fear motivated me.

Teachers dealt with the daily problems: control the children, teach them, deal with their individual personalities. Bureaucrats dealt with: student-teacher ratios, dollars and cents, pensions, the administrivia of a school system. All these things, I felt, lost sight of the school's main priority—the children. It was evident that staff and parents were afraid of change. Only Laini and I seemed to have our daughter's best interests at heart, all the time.

I remember the question: Do you read to her every night? Every night! Laini and I were avid readers. Our home resembled a library. Stephanie had an overflowing bookcase in her room. From the day she was born, we read with her. The teachers and bureaucrats searched for blame and pointed it in our direction, putting our emotions on a roller-coaster ride. Fortunately, this misdirection did not work.

I learned from my accident that crisis promotes growth. Thinking and taking responsibility for myself made my recovery possible. Once

I accepted Stephanie's crisis into my life, I stopped listening to the professionals and began listening to my soul instead. I applied the lessons of my past to my daughter.

Quickly, Stephanie was put on drugs to stabilize her sagging spirits and self-esteem. This was seen as a short-term solution to the problems that multiplied daily. While this was happening, I began reading and thinking. What caused her problem? Why were so many children being diagnosed as learning disabled in our school system?

I discovered that this problem was not isolated to our school alone. In some respects, it had taken on epidemic proportions across North America. Something was terribly wrong.

I went back to basics, the ones I examined during my recovery. The answer hinged on a theory I developed: the children were toxic-sensitive to our environment.

Millions of years of human evolution had been radically assaulted by the changes brought on by our modern Western societies. The simplest food, an apple or banana, was impregnated with chemicals. Potato chips, the snack food the school offered during its biweekly lunch program, was laden with fats and chemicals. As far as the water we drank, there could be times when the filtration systems failed, yet we still kept drinking it. The list of chemicals tested for in the water is just as important as the list of chemicals they do not test for. The children spent more time passively watching TV and movies than actively learning, playing or exercising. The problem was simple: improper lifestyle and misdirection of resources!

The crisis of my daughter's problem forced me to keep searching. The Great Ormand Street Hospital study of Great Britain found a link between hyperactivity and the food and water children consumed. Many parents and the school board resisted further examination of this problem, even after it was brought to their attention.

The crisis made me realize the quality of our children's lives was at stake. This awareness meant independent thinking and perseverance could be rewarded with results, and they were, in the case of my child. Hopefully, all the children will one day enjoy the fruits of my labors. I will know that the school board has focused again on its students when I see "Eat Your Way To Health Day" become a reality.

At home, I changed the kitchen into a user-friendly model that was back to basics. I did not ban junk food, preferring to use the kitchen as an interactive learning environment for the family.

Stephanie went off medication that summer. Her mind and body, stabilized by the drugs, were given a chance to heal without them. She is nine now, and does not take any drugs. Her marks and attitude are improving. Her acceptance of her problem is creating one heck of a great kid. Yes, she still is learning disabled. I prefer to think of her as being learning *enabled* and the seeds of her struggles are growing a happier, more fulfilled child each day. The crisis of Stephanie's learning disability is building a better person.

There are many types of crises in today's world. For example, in the late '70s and early '80s, New Zealand was faced with an economic crisis. The entire country plunged into chaos as the government dealt with its problems. But economic accountability was restored to the system through massive realignment of the economy. Today, New Zealand shows signs of a vibrant country. Its population survived and thrives.

Many years ago, North American car manufacturers faced a crisis brought on by complacency. Xerox faced a crisis when it lacked direction in the '80s. Innumerable companies went bankrupt during the last recession. Those who accepted and dealt with the crisis they faced are better for it. Today, North America produces top-quality cars. Xerox thrives as it constantly redefines its mandate. You, the consumer, are the winner.

Accept crisis into your life, learn from it; you will prosper and grow!

Exercise:

Think back to a crisis you resolved. When it was happening, how did you feel? Now that it is over, how do you feel?

By examining your past, you will realize that the crisis in your life, when treated as a learning experience, made you a better person.

Make a list of positive outcomes that occurred and what you learned from the crisis. Save the list for the next time you face a crisis; it will put things in perspective. You will survive and thrive, just as you did in your past. *Crisis builds character.*

Affirmations—repeat these to yourself frequently throughout the day:

- *"I accept crisis into my life as a learning experience."*
- *"I grow from within, when faced with crisis."*
- *"Crisis makes good outcomes possible."*

Chapter 27

Let Go of the Past

Let the poo-poo of your past become the fertilizer for your todays so that you may build a better tomorrow. Start doing this now. Do it repeatedly until it becomes second nature. It is a form of forgiveness that recognizes all was not well in your past, but says that it is okay today.

As I write this book, I relive each and every painful moment of my life. Tears well up in my mind, body and soul. I become moody and sad. I start smoking again at a furious rate. Revisiting my pain and anger takes a toll on me, but it is worth every bit of uneasiness. I have to let go of the past by choice, but I revisit it so I may share with you the valuable lessons I learned, one more time.

"Look how far you have come," I think as I create this legacy, my book, for my children and for you. The junk of the past has become wonderful material on which to build a new present and head toward a bright future.

Yes, I still have pain, but now it is my friend. When I am ill, it is my early warning system that enables me to take preventative actions. When the weather changes, I feel it in my body and prepare to welcome nature's gift. Pain lets me know I am alive.

No longer do I run from the pain of the past, but I bring it into my present, knowing that it has much to teach me every moment of my life.

My daughter is a wonderful teacher. At the age of nine she said, when I was experiencing the emotional pain of separation and divorce, "Daddy, the changes are over with, my brother and I can get on with our lives and make new friends." It was the simplicity and clarity of her statement that helped me realize my marriage had given me two beautiful gifts—Stephanie and Alan. My past had built a wonderful healing present. My daughter's presence of mind, in addition to her warm and comforting ways, was example enough. My children are a gift I always treasure and learn from. They are a perfect example of my past having a positive effect on my present!

Thomas Edison, the inventor of the light bulb, gave a wonderful example of letting go of the past. One day he was being interviewed by a newspaper reporter. The reporter, having done his homework, knew Mr. Edison had failed more than a thousand times to make a light bulb and he asked Mr. Edison about this.

"I learned over a thousand ways not to make a light bulb," was Mr. Edison's reply. Your past is a learning experience upon which you can grow a new you each day.

Exercise:

Close your eyes and go back to the time when you were just learning to read.

Remember when you started reading how difficult it was to tell the letters apart and sound out the words? How it seemed to take forever for you to grasp each word? How at first the pictures interested you more than the words?

Maybe the book was about Dick, Jane and Spot, or Big Bird, or a prince and princess. You struggled at first and possibly cursed, yet today you are reaping the rewards of the struggles of your past as you read the newspaper, a novel, this book.

Now that was an easy exercise. Start applying this thinking to all the events in your past. You can use your imagination and figure out how those events helped you survive and grow as a person. The key is to find out what positive value they added to your life. Burn your finger once, and I am sure you will be careful in the future not to do it again.

Affirmations—repeat these frequently to yourself throughout the day:

- *"My past is the basis for a new improved me today."*
- *"My mind finds good things of value in all that has happened to me."*
- *"I have a past that is the foundation for building a better me, today."*

Chapter 28

Abundance Versus Scarcity

Abundance—having more than enough—is a wonderful thing. There is more than enough in our universe. Unfortunately, most of us feel we do not have enough, which is a scarcity mentality. Accept the idea of abundance into your life, and your life will be enriched.

Unconsciously, I struggled with my scarcity mentality for 40 years of life. Only when I understood where this attitude came from could I deal with it. Even now, I occasionally slide back into the mentality of scarcity. When I use my awareness to free myself of thoughts of scarcity, my world is richer.

I was struggling at work, in real estate sales, feeling addicted to the money and people contact, but not feeling fulfilled. I was driving my car and the pleasant tingling feelings I had had since age 11 started to happen. I pulled over to the side of the road, closed my eyes and took some time out.

A thought hit me: I came from a poor family. And I had never realized this before. That thought set my direction in life. It was true, we were poor, but I had never known it. I was 16 when my dad, at age 44, moved out of the home his mother owned.

I called my mom to confirm this insight.

" . . . but you had lots of love," Mom said.

She was right. I did have an abundance of love.

I understood now why Dad took my sister and me for numerous drives through poorer areas of town. In his way, he was telling us to be thankful for the abundance in our lives. I only wish he were alive today so I could tell him I had all that I needed, and then some. I loved him then, now and forever. Love is so many things—one of which is the abundance that holds the universal intelligence together. Love is my definition of the universal intelligence, God.

I made an equation to show where this scarcity attitude came from, so I could focus on the present and the abundance around us:

Scar City + Scare City = Scarcity Mentality

This is what it means:

"Scar City" refers to the scars of my past, my childhood.
"Scare City" refers to the hidden fears, of not having enough, inside me.

Add the two together and you get a scarcity mentality. The equation helped me focus on the parts of my past causing those thoughts. I was finally free of them.

Children practice scarcity in their homes, at school and play. "What is mine is mine, what is yours I want!" is the schoolyard cry. Children compete for possessions, affection—even love—the most basic of needs. This is reinforced by their need to be accepted by their peers, sometimes at the horrible price of conformity that causes drug use, theft, vandalism and a host of other problems.

Where did my children learn these attitudes and coping mechanisms?

I looked in the mirror and saw where: me. At first, the idea hurt. But once I dealt with my attitude, it became a foundation to build upon.

I remember going for a walk with my son when he was four years old. He had candies, and whenever he met other children, he would stop and give them one. He shared his world of abundance and was quickly rewarded with acceptance from those he met.

Alan loves people, and people love him. Abundance says that there is more than enough in our universe. Alan practices this attitude, and so can you. Share your abundance with others.

I was asked to share a special word for a Toastmasters meeting this past December. This helps expand the vocabulary of the speakers. The word I chose was "paradigm."

The night before, I wrote "paradigm" on a large sheet of paper to put on the wall for everyone to see. On my way to the meeting, I realized it was Christmas, and I had "a shift in thought." Which, incidentally is what paradigm means.

I stopped at a store and got a roll of pennies. I hurried home and put the pennies in a container, which I labeled, **"Take 2 Pennies."** I headed back to the meeting.

I was just in time. I got up to make my presentation, and told the audience I had originally chosen the word "paradigm," but the holiday spirit caused me to have a shift in thought. I went to the blackboard and wrote H.O.P.E.

It stood for "Happiness Of People Expands." I asked each person to take two cents and share the abundance with others.

I told them how lucky I felt, since I was a child, whenever I found a lucky penny. Now I wanted to share the abundance I had in my life with the audience. I asked them to share it with others.

How?

"Throw away the pennies in places where others would find them," I said. Now you see how H.O.P.E. works, any season of the year.

Exercise:

Get some pennies or nickels. Find a relatively busy place and drop them. If you really want to see what sharing your abundance does, go somewhere and wait. Watch the delight on a child's or adult's face when they find your coin. It brings pleasure far greater than its worth, to both the giver and recipient.

Exercise:

This time find a partner. Tell them you want to demonstrate abundance with them. If they ask you what you mean, explain it to them. Ask them if you can hug them. If they say yes, do it! I bet you will both feel better for having shared your abundance.

Share your abundance with those you like and love and with the world at large, today.

Affirmations—repeat these frequently to yourself throughout the day:

- *"I live in a world of abundance."*
- *"I am thankful for all I have, and share my abundance with others."*
- *"I love the abundance of friends, family and people in my life."*

Chapter 29

Persistence Pays

Persistence is striving to succeed in the face of opposition. Winston Churchill summarized it by saying, "Never. Never. Never. Never give up!" This elegant definition of persistence was successfully demonstrated by the British and their allies in World War II. They won against seemingly impossible odds.

During my accident and recovery, I never gave up on myself. I discovered persistence comes from within. When I realized the effects of food and lifestyle on my daughter's learning disability and on children in general, I decided her classmates and school should become better educated about healthier choices. I created stories for the children.

One was about The Medicine Cabinet for Life—Kit. Stephanie helped me convert a medicine cabinet into a person, complete with arms, legs, face and hair. Kit was filled with shiny pictures of fruits and vegetables. One of the food characters was The Magic Toothbrush—Fibby, commonly known as fiber. Fibby explained how some foods clean the inside of the body. It caught the imagination of her classmates. Stephanie and Alan talked about Kit, Fibby and the food family for weeks.

The following story caught the imagination of all the boys and girls in their class. It was the story of a young child and a YO-YO Top called *The YO-yo-YO-yo-YO-yo Kid Kal—Keeps on Bouncing Back.* This adventure story inspired a host of comments like: "When is the kid going to Hollywood?" and "I will never give up in something I believe." Pretty remarkable for seven- and eight-year-old children. It did not end in the classroom. Alan and Stephanie kept asking me to tell the story. Finally, I wrote it down so Stephanie could read it to Alan.

The YO-yo-YO-yo-YO-yo Kid Kal—Keeps on Bouncing Back is my gift to all children. Kal is genderless in my rendition of the story. The reason is that both boys and girls must overcome adversities daily. As do you and I.

Exercise:

Your persistence will be practiced and demonstrated to the children in this exercise.

Watch the children show you persistence in action—they are masters of overcoming adversities.

Step 1

Read the story to your children or a friend's children. When you finish reading, ask them if they want to draw pictures for it. If they say yes, continue to step two.

Step 2

Over a few days, write the text on paper, leaving lots of blank space on each page for the children to draw on. I suggest you put each section on a separate page. Let the children fill in the blank spaces, any way they want to. It's lots of fun!

The YO-yo-YO-yo-YO-yo Kid Kal—Keeps on Bouncing Back
(As told by Ken to his daughter's third-grade class.)

★ ★ ★

This is the story of the YO-yo-YO-yo-YO-yo Kid . . .
Maybe you know this kid?

The kid could be your neighbor, your cousin, your friend, your brother, or sister . . . *or*

The kid could even be you!

★ ★ ★

This amazing tale is about one kid's struggle to overcome the tough things that happen to kids in their daily lives.

Kal won the struggle against the Earth's pull. Kal went from crawling . . . to standing . . . walking and at last to running!

Like a bumble bee . . . zip . . . zip . . . zipping all around, Kal moved around the ground. Until . . .

Uncle Bob and Auntie Lil came for a visit. Kal got a surprise in a little box.

★   ★   ★

Kal giggled and ripped the box open. Inside was a little round wooden thing with a string in the middle.

Kal tried to eat it . . . roll it . . . bounce it . . . throw it. Finally Kal gave it back to Uncle Bob.

Uncle Bob laughed and put the string around his finger, holding the wooden thing in his hand.

★   ★   ★

Suddenly Uncle Bob threw the round wooden thing on a string at the ground.

The round wooden thing stopped just before the ground. Spinning fast at the end of the string. Making a *zzz* . . . *zzz* . . . *zzzing* sound!

Kal's eyes opened wide with surprise at the dancing disc on the end of the string, making its magical sound.

Giggles of glee were heard and everyone joined in Kal's delight. Auntie Lil said, "Kal, it is a YO-YO." In an up-and-down voice for all to hear, Kal said, "YO-yo-YO-yo-YO-yo."

★   ★   ★

Uncle Bob put the string on Kal's finger. Kal threw the YO-YO to the ground and it went *kerplunk*. Kal looked sadly at the YO-YO as it lay on the ground.

Auntie Lil said, "Kal, when you're as tall as the red fire hydrant over there on the grass, the YO-YO will not go *kerplunk* anymore. It will dance in the air, at the end of the string, going *zzz . . . zzz . . . zzzing* just for you."

Mommy, Daddy, Uncle Bob and Auntie Lil sat on chairs on the porch. Talking and drinking water. Meanwhile . . .

★   ★   ★

Kal walked over to the red fire hydrant, holding the YO-YO in one hand and climbed up the hydrant to the top. Kal threw the YO-YO to the ground. It went *kerplunk.*

Mommy, Daddy, Uncle Bob and Auntie Lil ran to get Kal off the fire hydrant. Daddy said, "Kal, when you're big enough to ride a two-wheel bicycle, I will give you back your YO-YO top."

★   ★   ★

Kal grew and grew and grew up a lot. One day Daddy and Mommy got him a big bike with training wheels on it. Kal looked at the bike and asked, "Where is my YO-YO that comes with my bike?"

Mommy held the bike while Kal sat on it and waited for his dad to return with the YO-YO.

Dad returned with the YO-YO. He took Kal's hand and tied the YO-YO string around Kal's finger and helped hold the bike.

Kal threw the YO-YO to the ground and . . . it went *kerplunk*!

Mommy and Daddy said, "When you grow a little more, the YO-YO will work. Put it in your room until then."

Kal ran to the bedroom and hid the YO-YO in a drawer full of socks. Then Kal ran back outside to play.

★   ★   ★

The days passed and became months. Kal grew bigger and bigger. Then one day while riding the bike *up* and down . . . *up* and down . . . *up* and down grassy hills, Kal fell onto the grass and rolled down the hill.

Kal remembered the YO-YO rolling on the ground, quickly got up and pedaled the bicycle home. Kal ran to the sock drawer, got the YO-YO and ran outside.

Kal tied the string onto a finger. Threw the YO-YO to the ground and . . . it danced in the air going *zzz . . . zzz . . . zzzing* all around. Surprised, Kal pulled up the hand with the YO-YO string in it.

A shock of surprise and giggles of delight came from Kal as the magic dancing YO-YO bounced back up.

Mommy and Daddy saw what happened, began to applaud and said, "Kal, you have done it. We knew you could, when the time was right. We are proud of you never giving up!"

So ends the beginning of this first adventure of Kal the kid, also known as . . .

The YO-yo-YO-yo-YO-yo kid, because Kal never . . . **Never . . . Never . . . Never Gives Up!!!**

★　　★　　★

Congratulations! You persisted in reading the story. Now share it with others.

Affirmations—repeat these frequently to yourself throughout the day:

- *"I will never, never, never, never give up in what I believe."*
- *"I believe I can succeed at whatever I want to."*
- *"I will persist and take into account the feelings of others in all I do."*

Chapter 30

All Knowledge Exists— This Is the Gift of the Universal Intelligence, God

All knowledge exists. What creates difficulties is our inability to uncover or accept into our conscious awareness this information. My awareness expanded once I willingly accepted the abundance of the universal intelligence, God, into my life. Once I unconditionally accepted God my feelings of wholeness came to fruition.

I was driving my five-year-old son to his baseball game when he asked me, "Daddy, what is that building?"

I saw a beautiful house of God in the direction he pointed. I pondered a moment and said, "Son, that is a building people make so that those who feel the need to go to a place for prayer, have one."

"Mmmm," he said. The answer was not complete enough for him, so I continued.

"I believe that God's house of worship is nature—the trees, birds, earth, sky and stars. Where do you think God is?" I asked.

"In my heart," Alan replied with the wisdom of a five-year-old in tune with his world. I felt a warm tingle inside. At the time, his answer seemed complete to me.

I recalled that during my struggles with pain, I found the greatest comfort when I acknowledged that God existed. I did not have scientific proof of this universal intelligence, God; just the miracle of faith. This devotion and awareness brought a tingling to my body. The more I thought about God, the stronger the tingling became until it was an automatic happening within me.

I was comforted by my belief in God. I heard that Alcoholics Anonymous and various groups that embraced the organization's 12-step program had enjoyed great success. A key was unconditional acceptance of God. Psychiatrists deal daily with alcoholics yet are not as successful as Alcoholics Anonymous. My curiosity was aroused.

The 12-step program was a very successful approach that validated my thoughts about the power of faith in the universal intelligence. I had stumbled upon this belief during my recovery from my accident. It worked for me.

The feelings I was confronted with made the most sense when I walked in conservation areas or parks lush with vegetation. I felt great inner peace and harmony—a sense of oneness with the universe. The distractions of society were banished from my mind.

I am not observant in the traditional sense of the word. I chose to follow my own path. This path is there for those who unconditionally accept God into their lives. I became a spiritual individual, awakened to this awareness during my human experience.

I explain the richness of this experience as learning to live in awe of the present. I let my senses and intuitions consciously become part of my life. I accepted as truth that God is always there.

All things fell into place when I realized that I am in the heart of God. My clarity and sense of purpose were heightened. Life took on a special meaning, it was a gift, a learning experience that would get me to the next point on the plane of my spiritual journey. At last, I felt complete inner satisfaction, the doubts banished, my fears put aside.

The universal intelligence had supplied humanity with all it needed to thrive. It was humanity's mission to uncover this. I sought answers by going back to basics, learning to listen to my mind, body and soul. The more closely I listened, the greater inner peace I experienced.

I realized that modern science and society needed help. My children were constantly becoming ill; the healing within was malfunctioning. I perceived the weakness of our last century as we embraced intrusive interventionist models. Our bodies, minds and souls could not adapt quickly enough and our children were paying a high price.

Willingly we pursued convenience, destroying God's gift, our world, in the name of progress. Balance had to be restored. We were destroying God's medicine cabinet for life: our forests, water, the earth we grow food in. Humanity was not evolving fast enough to cope with the changes. I reasoned that progress in modern terms meant immediate satisfaction of all wants and needs. This is not possible.

It took the crisis of my daughter's learning disability to make me realize there had to be a better way. Nature's abundance of riches was being ignored. I theorized that the increasing numbers of problems our children suffered—asthma, allergies, and learning disabilities too many to mention—was due to their bodies' sensitivity and inability to adapt. It shook me profoundly when I realized we were killing our children's quality of life. My theory is that children are suffering from "toxic sensitivity to the man-made world."

I struggled with this knowledge until the universal intelligence reminded me that my answer lay in going back to basics. God's home is a natural world of miracles.

Stephanie no longer needed medication once she started taking more walks, eating a healthier diet and learning to keep focused. The drugs had stabilized her; it was up to us to give her body and mind time to heal. By age nine, there were many positive changes in her personality and she enjoyed many more achievements. God's message of "back to basics" had been received, applied and worked.

All knowledge exists. It was my stubbornness that prevented its working for my benefit sooner. I reawakened to the lesson of my past—to trust the mind-body-soul connection with which the universal intelligence wisely endowed me. It enabled me to go farther along my spiritual path to fulfillment.

Exercise:

Put aside an hour for yourself. Leave the distractions of modern society. Go for a walk and savor God's gift to humanity—nature. Be embraced by its beauty. Be in awe of its wonder as you commune with nature and the universal intelligence.

Do this as often as possible. The more often you do it, the more in tune with your universe you will become.

Exercise:

If you cannot leave your home, plan a time for yourself.

Fill the tub with water, at a comfortable temperature.

Put on some gentle music that masks any outside noise. It could be the sounds of nature, like loons or whales, or sounds of silence that you more clearly hear when you close your eyes.

Get into the tub and savor its warmth.

Say to yourself, "All is well in my world."

Close your eyes and let your thoughts and feelings flow freely. Gently, let your mind, body and soul drift as they did in your mother's womb.

When you feel in touch with your inner self and ready to break the magic of the moment, do so, with the knowledge that all is well.

Affirmations—repeat these frequently to yourself throughout the day:

- *"All knowledge exists and I wish to become aware of this."*
- *"I enjoy the knowledge gained from my human experience."*
- *"The answers lie within me and are found all around me."*
- *"Thank you, God."*

Chapter 31

Accept Anger into Your Life

Anger is extreme distress and hostile feelings which usually surface as a result of hurt or opposition. That is a textbook definition. In fact, anger is hell!

Nearly dying made me angry, but the victimization and dysfunctional relationships that evolved from the incident got me *really angry*! So angry that it was difficult, and impossible at times, even to communicate my feelings to others. Other people did not know how to deal with my anger, and I assume they had not learned how to deal with their anger.

Their turning away from me was a passive form of opposition to my anger, which just made things worse. I got angrier and angrier. Eventually, all this anger turned inward, and I became depressed. Depression turned to anxiety, and anxiety caused more depression. The cycle seemed never ending.

I discovered I dealt with anger by copying the models from my childhood. My dad dealt with his extreme frustration by becoming angry and yelling. For him, it was a release; for me, it was the dysfunctional way I learned to deal with my anger. Fortunately, I survived and broke free of this vicious cycle.

I took a series of seminars with others who were angry. I discovered triggers that made me angry. During these groups, I was repeatedly asked, "Why are you here? Are you angry?" When I signed up for the group, I was angry, but I made a commitment to myself to deal with my anger. I learned how to accept anger into my life, and understood that it was my problem.

Finally, the "deep inside me" healing began. I made a list of things that got me angry. It was very extensive. Then I chose the top three triggers that set me off, and imagined positive ways to deal with each of them before they happened.

I used to get angry when someone lectured me about smoking. I was upset by these uninvited intrusions into my space that I perceived curbed my freedom. Intellectually, I agreed that smoking is bad. Emotionally, I rebelled against this opposition by yelling or shutting people out. My decision led me to a fascinating discovery.

People were right: smoking hurt me. Finally, I intellectually and emotionally accepted this. I made a conscious choice to keep smoking until I was ready to quit. I told others of my decision. I acknowledged their concerns by saying, "Thank you for caring."

Using these two strategies, I was able to deal with a situation that angered me. I stopped trying to defend the behavior. I acknowledged its negative impact and started dealing positively with it. Those who kept imposing their opinions on me accepted my position. I no longer got angry.

Taking the trigger for my anger and deciding beforehand what to do had an added bonus. I became less stressed and could stop smoking for weeks and months at a time. The need to smoke started decreasing. I had learned to accept my anger into my life and deal with it.

When I began writing this book, I decided to start smoking again. I have only one fully functioning lung and knew it was not a wise decision. The choice I made was my way of beating up on myself, as I relived the details of my near death, pain and suffering. All the rationalization in the world never makes a bad choice better, yet consciously choosing to smoke helped me deal with the feelings I revisited during the writing.

Next week, I am quitting again, I hope forever, since I no longer let anger and other negative emotions unconsciously trigger my reactions. Anger takes many forms, some subtle, some not. I learned to use my anger to help promote my healing.

My children used to yell, scream, kick, hit—the list of ways they dealt with anger was endless. I applied the trigger approach in a variety of ways. First I asked them to take time out, by them-selves—something I did for myself when I got angry. This gave them the opportunity to settle down emotionally.

I asked them to think of two better ways they could deal with the situation that angered them, while they took their time alone. When they were ready, they told me their better ways of dealing with their anger.

Thinking of positive outcomes before bad situations recur makes them valuable learning experiences. I proudly say I have a six-year-old and nine-year-old who are learning a variety of coping skills to deal with difficult times. This is part of my legacy to them.

The applications of these ideas reach far beyond anger. I have seen people get angry over returning merchandise to stores. The price they pay, in terms of unnecessary stress and usually failure to achieve their objective of getting satisfaction, carries over into other parts of their lives. The forcefulness anger promotes destroys the quality of life.

Someone returning an obviously used item approached the clerk in such a charming way that the clerk accepted it as a return. They told the clerk the item had been worn, apologized for bringing it back, and told the clerk they knew the store usually sold better quality merchandise than the item they had bought. The customer asked the clerk to bring the merchandise to the store owner's attention and give them a receipt for it, so they could get it back once it had been examined by the store owner.

You should have seen the flabbergasted look on the clerk's face. She replied that she did not want to inconvenience a good customer like him any further, then proceeded to give the customer a credit note for the goods. Everyone was happy. I believe this customer will return to the store and, ultimately, the store owner will be rewarded many times over.

Cynics might say the customer will take advantage of the clerk and store again. They might be right. Next time a situation occurs where you can either yell or charm the clerk, practice preventative anger management and use charm. See the results when you use charm and sincerity. Pat yourself on the back for a job well done. Your children will learn from this, and more important, you will be happier in the long run, having enhanced the quality of your life.

Exercise:

Find a quiet place. Get comfortable. Think of something that makes you angry—kids, spouse, politics, paycheck, whatever triggers your anger—and picture it in your mind.

Now picture a different outcome. Let's say it is your spouse criticizing you that ticks you off. Next time, picture yourself thanking them for criticizing you. Acknowledge their right to feel and say what they wish. Accept this negative into your life and deal with it. Learn from it. You will live a better and happier life.

Affirmations—repeat these frequently to yourself throughout the day:

- *"I accept anger into my life and learn from it."*
- *"I choose not to be angry, but to think of positive outcomes to opposition."*
- *"I am not angry. I am happier for dealing with my anger in positive ways."*

Chapter 32

The Healing Touch

The word "healing" means to become healthy or well again. It refers to the process of mending or curing a condition that is unhealthy to your well-being. The word "touch" means coming in contact with something, either directly or at a distance. When you combine the two, you get the healing touch.

During my recovery, I went to a masseuse and a lady of the night to receive the healing touch. This reaffirmed my body's wholeness to me by allowing me to feel human contact without hidden agendas. Unconditional contact or contact where the boundaries were clearly defined allowed me to reunite with my body, mind and soul. Physical touch enabled my body to be a vehicle for reuniting my mind-body-soul connection.

This awareness created a new perception of my world. I realized that the old model of the brain, therefore my mind, being in my body, was a dysfunctional model. In truth, my body was in my mind. The power of the mind to guide and control my body and thoughts became evident to me. The healing touch helped me realize that the body is in the mind.

When either of my children are distressed, if they allow me to, I hug them. More important, I hug them whenever I can, no matter their state. Before they go to bed, when we greet each other—the opportunities for hugging are boundless. This is more comforting to them and me than all the words I can say. I noticed how quickly, as babies, they quieted when held and cuddled.

Last year, my widowed mother became a volunteer cuddler at a local hospital. At age 65, she was a surrogate mother. The premature babies benefited immensely. Mom benefited as it had been 18 years since my dad had passed away and to my knowledge this lovely woman had not bonded with anyone else since her husband's death. The medical system was realizing the healing power of touch.

Science and medicine are discovering the curative effects of touch. Studies indicate some people have greater healing touch powers than others. In a double-blind study of people with recently broken bones, those who received the healing touch from people adept at it healed more quickly. The power of touch is becoming more evident each day.

Whenever someone I know is in mourning, if they allow me, I embrace them. A good hug does more than any words I could say. The awareness of the power of the healing touch helped me create my personal guidelines for daily hugs. Hugs are vitamins for my mind-body-soul connection. They add quality to my life. These are my requirements. They vary by person. You may have a different set of needs. Discover them.

Ken's Daily Hug Chart

Three hugs a day for minimal sustenance of self. It leaves you thirsty.

Six hugs a day for nurturing. You feel quenched but still unsatisfied.

Nine hugs a day for regular growth. Feels good.

Twelve-plus hugs a day for inner, outer and spiritual growth. It stores some away for those occasional hugging lapses. Your mind-body-soul will know this.

Exercise:

Make your own daily hug chart. Start with one hug a day and build your own guidelines for sustenance, nurturing, growth and super-growth bank-it-away purposes. Remember to get permission beforehand from those you wish to hug and be hugged by.

Exercise:

If no one is nearby, wrap your arms around yourself and give yourself a big hug.

Continue until you feel satisfied and nurtured.

Exercise:

Upon greeting friends, ask their permission to share a hug.
Once received, go for it.

Affirmations—repeat these frequently to yourself throughout the day:

- *"I love to hug and be hugged."*
- *"I feel the power of the healing touch."*
- *"When I ask for and get permission to hug and be hugged, I feel great."*

Chapter 33

Awakening to Being Human—As an Excuse

"Damn! I messed it up. Oh, well, I am only human." I have often heard others say that. Apologizing for their humanness. Using their human experience as a reason for making mistakes. I believe being human is a gift, the one that the universal intelligence, God, gives us.

You and I were given a mind, body and soul. It is easy to accept the idea that you have a body. You wake up, eat, play, make love and do an infinite amount of activities that daily reaffirm the existence of your body. You watch TV, read the newspaper, curse at the taxes you pay and perform an infinite number of activities on a conscious and subconscious level that reaffirm you have a mind.

In our perception, the mind resides in our brain, which rests in our bodies. As long as I accepted that idea, I kept suffering the pains that had resulted from my accident and from life itself. Once I understood that the mind is not in the body, but that the body is in the mind, I was able to make progress. This perception allowed me to find the source of the ultimate power, which is within each of us. No longer did I need to use my humanness as an excuse, since I understood it to be a gift, the fullness of which I began to discover.

Acknowledging that I had a soul became important to my well-being. I searched within myself, going back to the beginning of my conscious awareness, to discover that my soul, or spirit, existed before my mind and body did. My soul is a part of the universal intelligence—like a cell is to the body. My human experience was a manifestation of my soul. It hit me that I am a spiritual being having a human experience. It was an awesome awakening, brought on by the simplest of events, the death of a jade tree.

This occurred at the beginning of my journey into self-awareness, but it was over a decade later before I fully accepted soul into my reality. That is when I truly realized I was experiencing a celebration of life.

At the end of this key is the short story, "The Awakening." It details the nature of events leading to making this awareness part of my reality.

Alan was four and Stephanie was six when we went for a walk in a conservation area. Their natural curiosity showed itself as they giggled, ran, laughed and explored nature's wonders. They stopped by a stream and began to look for fish. Suddenly, Stephanie's shoes were off and she waded into the shallow water, trying to catch an elusive minnow. Alan followed quickly behind, shoes still on.

I felt like a kid again and joined them by the riverbank. My children were teaching me a valuable lesson: life is to be experienced. Intuitively, children reach out to the world around them in search of meaning. I discovered that it is more important to show them life than to tell them about it.

Descartes, the great French philosopher, took a reductionist approach to life. He reasoned that knowledge was best gained by trying to reduce our existence to the most basic component. He was a forefather of the Western world's scientific reductionist model. This approach cuts out the distractions around you to produce an intense focusing. Colds and infections are caused by virus or bacteria. The root cause of the problem is reduced to its smallest component. Today the scientific world uses Descartes' thinking as the basis for our scientific approach to life. It is a narrow focusing that causes people to unintentionally discard what they cannot answer.

It ignores a very basic point—healing occurs from within. The external focus, a scapegoat mentality of health care—causes us to empower others. In fact your mind-body-soul connection is the greatest healing mechanism.

In our quest for answers, our humanness becomes the excuse for not looking at the broader picture of the mind, body and soul.

In Far Eastern religions, philosophies and medicine, this is not the case. The Far Eastern model encompasses all aspects of our perceptions of humanness. It includes the mind-body-soul connection as one entity that is required for healing.

In the healing professions, Western society is incorporating many of the Far Eastern approaches to healing. Scientific research is beginning to focus on the healing properties of food, herbs, spices and essential oils. We are incorporating the best of all worlds into a universal approach to our health care.

Israel's Volcani Centre at Beit Dagan explores the healing properties of nature's medicine cabinet for life: herbs. The active ingredient in feverfew—parthenolide—helps migraine sufferers, especially when taken under medical supervision. Galilee Herbal Remedies of Kibbutz Kfar Hanassi grows the world's most potent supply of this herb and exports it to numerous companies.

Far Eastern societies never gave up the practice of using nature's gifts as enhancements to healing. They incorporate mind-body-soul concepts into their medical practices. Acupuncture and meditation are just two of the methods. Western society is incorporating these into its health-care systems. Bill Moyers, in his PBS series *Healing and The Mind*, explores the connections between mind, body and soul. He explores the diversity of Oriental approaches in contrast to Western methods in the practice of medicine. Research and medical science is now helping us understand these diverse approaches to healing.

We are witnessing a renaissance that acknowledges the universal intelligence's gifts to humanity. In terms of you and me, this means "The Celebration of Life" we experience during our human portion of our spiritual journey is blossoming.

Being human is not an excuse, it is the acknowledgment of our human adventure, a truly grand gift!

Exercise:

Write a note to yourself, saying, "I enjoy my human experience." Place it by your bedside before you fall asleep. When you wake up, read the note. Close your eyes and savor the sensations your mind and body are experiencing. Slowly stretch your body, feel one by one the sensations of your muscles awakening and coming to life. Inhale deeply, hold your breath, then exhale through your mouth and taste the air. Open your eyes and drink in the abundance of light and colors that greet them. Living in awe of the moment is what your human experience is about. It is a truly sensual adventure.

Exercise:

Take time and go for a walk. Smell the flowers. Touch the trees. Take your shoes off and run your toes through the earth. Enjoy your humanness today!

Affirmations—repeat these frequently to yourself throughout the day:

- *"I love my human experience."*
- *"I accept my mind and body as part of my spiritual journey."*
- *"I love life."*

The Jade Tree: On Awakening to Your Human Experience

(Text of Dramatic Speech presented to New Horizons Toastmasters)

"Damn you," I yelled at my wife on our 16th anniversary. *"It is not a bonsai tree! The bastard cheated you! Don't you . . . "* Laini, my wife, and Stephanie, my seven-year-old, had searched for a bonsai tree as my anniversary gift.

Crassulas arborescenes, better known as the Chinese jade tree, has a thick stubby trunk that holds it up. Its roots, like those of the cactus, reach deep down into the earth, searching for water. They suck water up into the fleshy gray-green round leaves that look like flattened balloons. In these leaves the water is stored until needed. When you look at jade trees, these stubby succulents give you a sense of inner peace, if you let them, but only if you are aware of their struggles.

Jade trees have a special meaning for me. Years ago, between surgeries to repair my partially paralyzed body, I received one as a gift. At first, it flourished with the multitude of other plants my wife, the nurturing gardener, cared for. I refused to have anything to do with the plants. They made me feel sad, since plants, like people, die.

When I had my accident, I touched the hand of death, found it wanting me, but I was not ready to die.

During my recovery, I was grappling with the physical and emotional pain of seeing part of my body slowly dying a little bit more each day. Atrophy had set in. At first my arm just hung there. As the process continued, biceps, once young and strong, melted away. They were useless and dying. They felt like jelly. The jade tree had become a symbol of life for me, struggling to survive and somehow thriving in a hostile universe.

Laini and I had been married five years at the time of the accident. She tended her garden and my jade tree, with the gentle loving care of a woman who would one day bear our children. Daily she diligently said "Hello" to her plants, watering them and showering them with loving care. They flourished. All, that is, except for the jade tree; it slowly shriveled up and wilted. Death was calling it.

No matter how much care and nurturing it got, the jade tree did not respond. The attempts at resuscitation—daily watering and talking to it—were to no avail.

"Laini, stop watering it. It's a succulent, you're drowning it," I yelled to deaf ears. Like a busy ant, she mindlessly tended to the plant.

"Leave it alone!" I begged. My pleas went unheeded.

This symbol of my struggles continued to drown in the tender loving care and water of my wife's ministrations. It was like the conditional love I was getting from those around me; it was attacking my soul. Finally, the jade tree died.

A little bit of me went with it to plant heaven. At last, it had escaped the hell of this world. At that time, in my heart, my secret wish was to die.

Sixteen years after our wedding, while we struggled to make our marriage survive, I was given the symbol of my death wish from the past. In my mind, I no longer was like the jade tree of long ago that I received after my accident. My wife was trying to show me that I had changed.

Unfortunately, I was blinded by my past anger and frustration, as it became part of my present when Laini gave me the jade plant as an anniversary gift. I had never fully dealt with the bond I felt ten years earlier, of my struggle to survive and the jade tree's struggle. To me that jade tree's death was symbolic of what I was going through then and ten years later, in our marriage.

"Why do you relive the pain of your past sufferings?" you might ask.

Nine months after Laini had given me the jade tree as an anniversary gift, I apologized to her for my outburst. I celebrated my new awareness by buying myself a wonderful big jade tree, one that had grown as strong as I had in the past year. I had found a place inside myself of inner peace and harmony, made possible by the pains of my past.

I took the jade tree home and made a place for it. It had outgrown its pot. Lovingly, I mixed sand and soil. One part sand, two parts soil. Slowly, I filled the new pot. The texture of the earth and sand felt comforting between my fingers.

Gently, I removed the jade plant from its old pot, unwrapping it as a mother undresses her baby. To remove the jade from its pot, I cut the black plastic, trying not to hurt even one root. Swiftly and firmly I placed it in its new home, adding one handful at a time of the magic soil. I watched with satisfaction and completeness as the sandy soil sought out any gaps between the plant and pot. When this was done, I moved the jade tree into the kitchen, so it could catch the morning sun.

"No water until tomorrow," I said to it. " You need your rest."

Tomorrow became today. I got the watering can, ran the tap water until it was just right and filled the can. I drenched the jade from above, like a desert flash storm does. It was then that I noticed an unusual white spot.

I bent over, with the wonder of a child in my heart, and saw a tiny miracle. My new jade tree had given me a miniature white flower, as a thank-you. I sat down beside it and reminisced, of times past and present. I thought of my long-dead jade tree.

Much time passed before I awakened from my reverie. I looked at my watch and realized it was nine months to the day since I had yelled at Laini on our 16th anniversary. I got up and went to the jade tree anniversary gift. It sits on our fireplace mantel. Two stickers attached to its pot command: *"Do Not Touch!" "Do Not Water!"*

I reached out and removed them, at last, because I knew I had fully awakened to my human experience.

Life's adversities are many. How you choose to deal with them is the measure of your completeness as a human being. The sooner you awaken to your mind-body-soul connection, the fuller your life will be.

May today be the day you learn to live in the present, finally setting yourself free, at last, from your past. May today be the day you have your awakening.

Postscript: Laini and I are the proud parents of two wonderful children. We had grown apart and learned to accept this as we went our separate ways. Divorce became our healing relationship. The children are happy, healthy and better for having known Laini and me as husband and wife. This too is a part of the human experience of our spiritual journey. Now we have peace at last.

Chapter 34

Being Human—
On Becoming One
with the Universe

Being human means accepting that you are in crisis and pain. It means accepting that you have a mind, body and soul. The latter is most difficult for many people to accept since they cannot see, hear, feel, taste or touch their soul. The soul is your spiritual part, and your human experience is a learning experience for your spiritual being, a part of your spiritual journey.

You can become totally fulfilled by accepting the existence of your soul without the need for proof. You have everything to gain by accepting this, and nothing to lose.

Probably no human power could relieve your crisis and pain as well as your soul and God can. Seeking them is part of accepting them.

One night as I walked, I looked to the heavens and saw a shooting star. I realized that shooting stars are like spirits; they are energy that burns brightly for a moment, then fades. My human experience was a part of this awesome display of the universal intelligence's wisdom.

I live in an age of miracles, when the frontiers of Western medicine push back death's door. Death is part of the miracle of life. It is an overpowering part of my human experience, that helps me fulfill my soul's need to know of and accept God into my life.

Shortly after that walk, I experienced the depth of the fullness of the universe during a visit to my cousin Linda as she lay in a hospital dying. It was then that I wrote my epitaph and disguised it as hers, since I feared the recriminations of those around me.

Being human means accepting the fullness of your life. I now share with you this story:

Linda's Song
Goodbye—The Epitaph

My name is Ken. I am compelled to first explain to you why I am sharing this story with you, how it came to pass and its unique style. Please excuse this feeble attempt at trying to recreate my last visit with my cousin Linda, age 47, as she lay dying on her hospital bed. Her struggle to survive cancer and the impoverished medical attempts at intervention prolonged her struggle. It was the egotistical conceit of those who stopped Mother Nature from reclaiming her child Linda, that led to this disjointed final meeting.

I use a unique combination of poetry and prose to reflect her life's ebb and flow. The sharing used her thoughts, emotions and speech. One moment the feelings poetically caressed my soul; the next, like a car in a skid, her speech changed direction. This is Linda's life story. The essence of her life: smooth, flowing and joyous at times, intermingled with moments of great emotional pain. It is a truly humbling and onerous task that is set before me, one which I feel inadequate about even attempting to fulfill, yet I am compelled to do so. I must share her last thoughts with you.

This story summarizes what Linda and I shared during my last visit with her, during this portion of her human experience. Her human experience is a part of her spiritual journey. It is a combination of poetry and prose, reflective of her life's ebb and flow.

This is the happiest moment of my existence. May it not be one of the saddest moments in your life . . .

At last I get the chance to finish my finest work. The conclusion is simple, you will see as you search inside yourself. I hope I touched your mind and found your heart wanting. My pen and paper, words so weak, caressed your soul on deep. Happily, wistfully I do say, "No longer do I play in the garden of humanity, for all to see. At last I am one with the universe, this is my final tomb. Please take a moment and reflect, the story I have won. So here it is, at last you see, my greatest work on high. When next you meet me, may there be, a twinkle in your eye. Live loving, love living, fear death not.

I have touched the hand of death, found it wanting and at last it took my lot. Living, loving, laughing . . .

So here at last is my conclusion: beginning, middle and end. The final story I shall write, is my greatest in the end. Just take this one-word story, in all its glory and remember that it means so much for you who are ready to receive it.

My final gift, is but this word, and all it encompasses. May it endure the past, present and future as I shall. Now for the single-word story, revealed in all its glory.

"One"

Finally I can rest, my work is done.

Exercise:

Seek inner peace and tranquillity as you savor the moments of your life.

Be kind and caring to those around you and do a "living will," which explains what you want to happen to you in case you are incapacitated; make a will for when you die.

These wills may be the final act of kindness you are remembered for. In this way, you are making life easier for those who survive you.

Affirmations—repeat these frequently to yourself throughout the day:

- *"I love the human experience of my spiritual journey."*
- *"I love living and live loving."*
- *"I am one with the universe."*

Chapter 35

Share What Has Happened

Sharing with others what has happened means talking to another person honestly and openly about your situation. The fullness of this is best found when you also share with God, the universal intelligence. These acts can be done in private, and there are many ways to accomplish them.

I was frustrated during my recovery from the parasailing accident. My wife and the health providers refused to accept what I told them—that I had died. They attributed my belief to delirium, since I had sustained a head injury; half my face had a scab and there was the possibility my left eye would be lost. This head injury made it easier for them to reject my sharing. Eleven years later, my wife told me I had not been breathing when I was taken out of the water after the accident. This was the first time she acknowledged that I had been technically dead. What had I done during the preceding years?

Psychiatrists, a hypnotherapist, a lady of the night and friends became part of my search for acknowledgment that I had died and been given a second chance. The search to find someone who listened without prejudging was trying and difficult.

Many times I walked the wrong path. But something inside me refused to give up. I found that being honest with myself and another person helped, yet it was not satisfying enough.

The tingling I felt occurred more often when I prayed to God. Intellectually I believed in God, yet emotionally had felt betrayed by this universal intelligence. At first, contact with the universal intelligence happened accidentally. Then it came easily, once I removed myself from the distractions of daily life and went for a walk in a park or the woods. The more I accepted God into my life, the more easy the sharing became.

One day, when Alan was five and we talked about God, he helped enlighten me by telling me that God was in his heart. Once I accepted that I was in the heart of God, my sharing took on a richness that left me with an inner peace and tranquillity. I felt whole again.

I combined the three parts of my revelation: be honest to myself, share with a friend and share with God. The approach worked to lessen my pain. It can for you, too.

Exercise *(This is a three-part exercise)*:

1. Make a personal accounting of the bad things that happened to you or that you have done in your past. Be honest and record your thoughts.

2. Find a friend who will accept without question or judgment what you share with them.

3. Find a place, any place: house of prayer, a park, a quiet place in your home and share with God what has happened.

Be patient with yourself and allow time for the sharing to happen.

Affirmations—repeat these frequently to yourself throughout the day:

- *"I am honest with myself."*
- *"I will find a friend and share with them what has happened to me."*
- *"I share my past with God."*

Chapter 36

The M.S.G. For Life—Death

After I died, I felt my life was on hold. For nine years, I struggled with my physical and emotional pain. At times, death was an alternative I welcomed. It was an escape from the daily horrors I faced inside myself. It was my final salvation, an option I could not share with others since I feared they would lock me up and throw away the key.

Knowing I had an escape route—suicide—made my life tolerable. To the outside world, I was okay. The turmoil was my little secret. Once I managed to deal with my pain to my satisfaction, I no longer looked at death as a solution. I looked at death as the M.S.G. flavor-enhancer for my life. Death indirectly motivated me to keep on going.

I shared the idea with others that death, since it is the final portion of our human experience, was my motivation. Knowing my physical life would come to an end gave me a sense of urgency. This meant my goals were important to me. I had to deal with my pain or die. I did not want to die in mind, body or soul.

From age 16, I started seeing people close to me die. My grandfather, a 25-year-old friend, a 21-year-old friend, my grandmother, my dad—the list kept getting longer. I was in my mid-20s when I concluded that death is the end of the human part of my existence. But it was my own near-death experience that made me realize death is not the end, just a stepping stone to the next part of your growth. I was awakening to my spiritual side, my soul.

My fascination with death led me to speak with older people about dying and death. As they neared death, its closeness kindled something inside them. It amazed me how many people in the later stages of life started consciously searching for their spiritual side. I asked myself, "Why wait to discover your soul?" I only discovered the answer once I had had my near-death experience. Death was the time clock I would punch at the end of my days on earth.

At age five, my daughter bought her first goldfish. It only lived a few weeks before it died. She went into mourning and performed a burial ceremony for the fish. She discovered that something she took for granted, life, was a fragile and precious thing.

Repeatedly, she bought goldfish; repeatedly, they died. It was a process of desensitization that allowed her to accept death as a normal part of living. The desensitization ended when my 47-year-old-cousin, Linda, died from cancer. This was a person my daughter knew and liked.

By the time Linda died, Alan was five years old and had shared Stephanie's goldfish experiences. His fascination with death manifested itself in wanting to see my father's grave when we went on vacation to visit his grandparents in Montreal.

It was the middle of winter when he and I went to the cemetery. There he stood, barely able to reach the top of my dad's headstone, when he reached down, took a stone and placed it on top. With a nod of his head, he muttered, "Goodbye." He turned and threw his arms around me and planted a big kiss on my cheek. Death had taught him to appreciate the living.

It may have been a cold, snowy and windy day at the cemetery, but for me the sun had shone. Even to a child, my son, death could hold a positive life-affirming message.

Exercise:

Buy a long-stemmed cut rose, with the flower closed. Put it in a vase. Give it sunshine, air and fresh water daily. Watch it blossom before your eyes. Savor its colors, textures and smell. Befriend it as you would a person.

Slowly, no matter what you do, the natural cycle of life takes over. The rose will start to wither, then die. Its beauty will be lost from your sight, forever.

Once the rose dies, cut it up into as many small pieces as you can. Take the parts to your garden and mix them with the soil. The dead rose will give back to the earth the hidden gifts it took while it was alive.

You knew the rose would die, no matter how much tender loving care you gave it. You savored its presence while it flourished. Now embrace the message the rose gave, that death is a naturally occurring event, not to be feared. Death allows you to accept the beauty and joy life offers while we are alive. Even in death, the rose adds beauty and meaning to life.

Exercise:

Buy a flowering bulb. Plant it according to the instructions. Care for it as required. In time, the miracle of life that is hidden beneath the surface of the earth will spring up. Nature will follow its course and just like the rose, beauty and joy will enter your life. Because you know the flower will die, you will savor it all the more.

Learn from this, that people are like flowers; we live to strive, to survive and thrive on a daily basis. Daily we die. Learn to treat others as you treat these flowers, and your life will be richer for it. Savor your life, each moment, understanding that death may snatch it from you at any second and you will have discovered how death is life's M.S.G., flavor-enhancer.

Affirmations—repeat these frequently to yourself throughout the day:

- *"I do not fear death. It makes my love of life richer."*
- *"I love life."*
- *"My life is a celebration I treasure."*

Chapter 37

Visioning Makes Your Dreams Become a Reality

Visioning is being able to create a mental image of what you want to become or to happen. In this context it refers to what you want to make of yourself. It is a state of conscious awareness in which you begin making your ideas into reality. Anyone who has a dream, thought or idea is bringing many elements of the keys contained in this book into practice. The fact that you are reading this is a good example of visioning. You saw the possibility that *The Ultimate Power* would improve your life. You had a vision and went about creating a new awareness and future for yourself. Congratulations on being a visionary!

When my daughter, Stephanie, was seven years old, she had trouble falling asleep. We started walking outside late at night. It was my vision of a healthy and happy child that enabled me to do this. Gradually, she started to fall asleep more easily.

One night she looked to the stars and said, "Star bright, star light. First star I see tonight. I wish I were I wish I might have my wish come true tonight." It is a beautiful way to do visioning.

I believe that one star and one wish a night are not enough. I reworded it to say, "Starssss bright. Starssss light. All the starssss I see tonight. Wishes are. Wishes might. Come true each and every night."

At first, Stephanie resisted the idea. Then her brother Alan and I started saying it together, and her resistance melted. Maybe my vision of a better world enables me to share my visions with you and my children. I believe *fate is what you make of it* and visions are one key to helping you fulfill yourself.

When I started creating my vision of a better world, I saw myself as a professional speaker and writer. I made a vision list and mission statements for the various projects I wanted to undertake. Here is a partial list of my visions. May you help me make them a reality:

- Do 10 major inspiring motivational keynote addresses a year to major health-care associations, companies and groups.

- Address the Anthroposophical (mind-body-soul medical practitioners) convention, in Switzerland, when the doctors next gather, in the year 2000.

- Become a better person, each day of my life.

- Write or cowrite 12 inspiring self-help books, using personal experiences as the underlying foundation of logic for each of them. The second book in the series, *The Ultimate Lovemaking Guide— Lesson's From the Deaths of Relationships / How to Unlock Your Mind-Body-Soul Potential at Play and in Bed* will be published Valentine's Day 1997. The third book, *The Ultimate Power Continues: More Lessons From a Near-Death Experience—How to Unlock Your Mind-Body-Soul Potential,* is scheduled for release in 1997. My first book of inspirational humor for a new age, called *Down Home Wisdom From a City Slicker,* is scheduled for release soon.

- I will tour the United States and Canada in 1995 and 1996, promoting my mission in life. In 1997 I will begin touring Europe, Australia and whatever countries my book will be sold in. My children will join me.

- In 1998 or 1999 I will take my children with me to tour the Middle East. The purpose will be to create a Peace Garden, symbolic of the Garden of Roses in Washington, D.C., where the peace accord was signed. You can make this a reality. Write your president or prime minister and the secretary general of the United Nations, telling them you support the idea of a Middle East Peace Garden—maybe it should be on the Golan Heights. Ask two friends and your children to help do the same. Give them an envelope with a letter to sign and mail. Ask each friend to ask two others to do the same thing, and so on. Share the vision and help make it a reality.

In the letter you could write: "Please fund and promote a Middle East Peace Garden. It acknowledges the dream of peace and creates a symbol for peace, for all children. I want it started by 1998 and run by the United Nations and all the countries in the Middle East. Thank you." (See Appendix for addresses.)

As you can see, my calendar of visions is filling up quickly.

- Write 12 inspiring children's stories. I have included one, *The YO-yo-YO-yo-YO-yo Kid Kal—Keeps on Bouncing Back*, about persistence. It is included in the book you are reading. It is my gift to you and the children.

- Produce 12 audio/video information works. In formats such as tapes/CDs/Digital Audio Tapes/Interactive Computer Programs. I am working on one called *The Gift of Laughter*. One side is of my children laughing and the other side contains affirmations for daily life and laughter exercises. It will be ready by fall of 1996. Laughter is a wonderful medicine that heals the mind-body-soul.

- Be invited to address the United Nations at the end of this millennium, as we begin the next one. I will do a short yet inspiring speech on peace and love.

  I wrote and received a letter back from the head translator at the UN, giving me some of the words I shall say, in 40 languages of the world. To coincide with my speech, I hope to arrange one minute of silent prayer for peace around the world—when not a gun is shot, no person maimed, no child is harmed. You and I can do it, for one minute. When it is done, how hard will it be for us to string the minutes into hours? Days? Years?

  It is time we showed the children a better world is more than just a dream.

- In my 53rd year of life, I will give myself a birthday present vacation and walk around the world, sharing my message of peace and love with one and all. Why?

  My father and grandfather died when they were 52. Each day of life beyond December 18 of my 53rd year of life is an extra special gift to me and those around me. This will be my way of giving back just a little more to this world than I have received from it.

  I started consistently exercising a year and a half ago. I walk or exercise for about an hour each day. Every three months I need new jogging shoes. I estimate I did 1,400 miles so far. It is a good start. It may take me longer than a year, but that is okay, I will be ready.

You are welcome to join me on my walk—in mind, body and soul. Together we can make a difference. We must show the children a better and peaceful world can be a reality.

When I created *The Love Living & Live Loving Series*™ and KeyPoint Guest Speakers, I created vision statements for each of them. This one I share with you:

The Love Living & Live Loving Series™ Statement

The Mission:

Share my mission of a better world/universe by using all available options.

Dear Friend,

The Love Living & Live Loving Series™ is dedicated to making our world a better place in which to live. Through sharing these magically mystical messages of the mind-body-soul connection, enlightenment for one and all is possible and probable.

Whether you read this book or any one of the other eleven in the series over the coming years, you will feel a greater sense of well-being and purpose. Your world will be forever richer for this.

It is the intention of the principal author, Ken Vegotsky, to directly share the abundance of this world, this universe with other writers and artists. I am dedicated and willing to share their message of inner peace and harmony using this gently enlightened fashion.

Each of the 11 writers may not even be consciously aware of the fact that they will be or are fulfilling their own deeply rooted mission in life, their purpose for being. I know who each of them is and at the appropriate time the message and mission shall be shared with them. They will join me in making this a better world.

Willingly they will come. Willingly they will share freely of themselves and their human experiences for the benefit of one and all. They are but servants of a greater presence that some call God, Mohammed, Vishnu, Buddha or Christ—and all those faiths that came before, during or after we shall have passed. It will occur to the writers and artists that they truly are spiritual beings having their human experience as part of their spiritual existence.

Ultimately all will be compelled to receive them into their homes in body, mind and soul. It is then that the fear of others will be lifted so that the mistiness that fogs their minds is also lifted. This series is not a threat to others' station in life but an enhancement of their desires for love, peace and brotherhood.

Neither this series nor its authors will desire or need to create another group, institution or religion based on their teachings. They will give freely of themselves and receive great profits in return so that they may continue to give freely of themselves and make this world a better place to be. It is for the benefit of the children that this must be done, and so shall it come to pass.

As humanity heads toward the light, on this plane of our existence, the struggles and perceptions of others may cause them to attempt an attack upon the principles shared in these writings. See that for what it is, their fear of enlightenment and inner need to control that which they see as a threat to their power.

Answer the doubters' fear with love and gentle kindness. This is the message of our universal intelligence. It binds all of us with the universe, in harmony. Answer their fear with charity, so that they shall not fear anymore. Answer their fear with love so that they may know the richness and fullness of our commonality.

So it is written and so shall it be . . .

Love,

Ken Vegotsky—August 20, 1994
Your perpetual student for life and teacher for a new millennium.

P.S. Visions are the seeds for your dreams. Your dreams are a stepping stone to a better today and tomorrow. It is not enough to tell the children we have a sacred mission; you and I must show them a better way to live. Only then can humanity arrive at its spiritual destination, together, as one.

Exercise:

Tonight, take a moment by yourself under the starlit sky. Close your eyes and open your mind, body and soul to finding visions for yourself. Use the "Starssss bright. Starssss light . . . " story above to give you focus. Share your visions with the stars, for they are the tears of joy of our universal intelligence.

Repeat this each and every night until your vision is crystal clear. When that moment has arrived, you will know it. It will be as much a part of your conscious awareness as is your body.

Exercise:

Take your friends and family with you, one at a time or as a group, and share the steps in the above exercise. Show them how to rediscover the child inside themselves.

Share your vision, so that they may share theirs, without fear of judgment.

Your mission is to go where few have gone before as you chart a new future for our world.

Affirmations—repeat these frequently to yourself throughout the day:

- *"I have a vision of a better today and tomorrow."*
- *"I love my visions."*
- *"I make my visions into dreams, and my dreams into reality, each and every moment of my life."*

The Mind-Body-Soul Connection

Dear Reader:

This final key to unlocking your mind-body-soul potential is a simple exercise.

Now you accept your human experience as part of your spiritual journey. You realize there is a mind-body-soul connection. It is time to complete your mission in life. Go forth and unconditionally share with others what you have learned.

Thank you for sharing this part of my journey with me. I leave you with this thought: "The journey of a thousand miles begins with the first step."

I beg to differ with our interpretation of Confucius. I believe the journey began long before you or I started our human experience. It is a spiritual journey, toward the light of our universal intelligence. Be embraced by its love.

Until we next meet.

Love,

Ken Vegotsky

Appendix

Addresses of Country Leaders

President of the United States of America
1600 Pennsylvania Ave., NW
Washington, DC 20050

Prime Minister of Canada
Parliament Building
80 Wellington St.
Ottawa, Ontario
Canada K1A 0A2

Prime Minister of Great Britain
10 Downing Street
London, England SW1 A2AA

Prime Minister of Australia
70 Phillips Street
Sydney, Australia 2000

Secretary General of United Nations
1 United Nations Plaza
New York, NY 10017

Organizations

This section is a small sampling of organizations and groups that can help you help yourself. Seek help and you shall find help. Never, never, never give up!

193

This sampling includes organizations promoting self-help as well as traditional and alternative-oriented health care providers—with an emphasis on the patients taking responsibility for their well-being. It is your responsibility to request this type of help and ensure that you receive what you ask for.

How to go about it:

These organizations can help you find traditional approaches, alternative health-care givers and self-help groups oriented to putting the emphasis on you taking responsibility for your well-being. If you want a Board-certified physician, you must specify that, as not all professionals are M.D.s.

These listings are not an endorsement, just a reference section of traditional, alternative heath care and self-help approaches you may explore. It is suggested that you consult with your Board-certified physician and have him or her monitor your status.

Note that these listings are accurate as of the date of original publication.

Please send a self-addressed stamped envelope with your queries. Be sure to ask for a referral if they cannot meet your needs.

Listings are by country—United States, Canada, Australia and United Kingdom.

The permanent worldwide headquarters of groups and associations are listed when they are mainly extensive networks of volunteers or local groups. First check your local phone book to find the local chapter's address and telephone number.

United States

Academy of Psychic Arts and Sciences
100B Turtle Creek Village, Suite 363
Dallas, TX 75219
(214) 788-1833

Academy of Religion and Psychical Research
P.O. Box 614
Broomfield, CT 06002-0614
(203) 242-4593

Alcoholics Anonymous World Service Inc. (First look in local phone book under Al-Anon)
P.O. Box 459, Grand Central Station
New York, New York 10163
(212) 870-3400

American Academy for Cerebral Palsy and Developmental Medicine
1910 Byrd Ave., Suite 100
P.O. Box 11086
Richmond, VA 23230-1086
(804) 282-0036

American Academy of Allergy and Immunology
661 East Wells St.
Milwaukee, WI 53202
(414) 272-6071

American Academy of Child and Adolescent Psychiatry
3615 Wisconsin Ave., N.W.
Washington, DC 20016-3007
(202) 966-7300

American Academy of Clinical Sexologists
1929 18th St., N.W., Suite 1166
Washington, DC 20009
(202) 462-2122

American Academy of Clinical Toxicology
Comparative Toxicology Lab
VCS—Kansas State University
Manhattan, KS 66506-5606
(913) 532-4334

American Academy of Environmental Medicine
P.O. Box 16106
Denver, CO 80216
(303) 622-9755

American Academy of Family Physicians
8880 Ward Parkway
Kansas City, MO 64114
(816) 333-9700

American Association of Naturopathic Physicians
P.O. Box 20386
Seattle, WA 98102
(206) 323-7610

American Academy of Health Care Providers
in the Addictive Disorders
260 Beacon St.
Somerville, MA 02143-3594
(617) 661-6248

American Academy of Medical Acupuncture
5820 Wilshire Blvd., Suite 500
Los Angeles, CA 90036
(213) 937-5514

American Academy of Medical Hypnoanalysis
25W 550 Royce Road
Naperville, IL 60565-8846
(800) 344-9766

American Academy of Neurology
2221 University Avenue S.E., Suite 335
Minneapolis, MN 55414
(612) 623-8115

American Academy of Orofacial Pain
10 Josplin Ct.
Lafayette, CA 94549-1913
(510) 945-9298

American Academy of Otolaryngic Allergy
8455 Colesville Rd., Suite 745
Silver Spring, MD 20910
(301) 588-1800

American Academy of Pain Management
3600 Sisk Road, Suite 2
Modesto, CA 95356-0549
(209) 545-0754

American Academy of Pain Medicine
5700 Old Orchard Road, 1st Floor
Skokie, IL 60077-1024
(708) 966-9510

American Academy of Physical Medicine and Rehabilitation
122 S. Michigan Ave., Suite 1300
Chicago, IL 60603
(312) 922-9366

American Acupuncture Association
4262 Kissena Blvd.
Flushing, NY 11355
(718) 886-4431

American Alliance for Health, Physical Education,
Recreation and Dance
1900 Association Drive
Reston, VA 66212
(703) 476-3400

American Art Therapy Association
1202 Allanson Road
Mundelein, IL 60060
(708) 949-6064

American Association for Cancer Research
620 Chestnut St., Suite 816
Philadelphia, PA 19106-3483
(215) 440-9300

American Association for Marriage and Family Therapy
1100 17th St. N.W., 10th Floor
Washington, DC 20036
(202) 452-0109

American Association for Music Therapy
P.O. Box 80012
Valley Forge, PA 19484-0012
(215) 265-4006

American Association for Therapeutic Humor
222 South Meramec Ave., Suite 303
St. Louis, MO 63105-3514
(314) 863-6232

American Association of Acupuncture and Oriental Medicine
433 Front St.
Catasaqua, PA 18032
(610) 433-2448

American Association of Behavioral Therapists
P.O. Box 1737
Ormond Beach, FL 32175
(904) 248-0508

American Association of Early Childhood Educators
3612 Bent Branch Court
Falls Church, VA 22041
(703) 941-4329

American Association of Naturopathic Physicians
2366 Eastlake Ave. East, Suite 322
Seattle, WA 98102
(206) 323-7610

American Association of Psychiatric Services for Children
1200 Scottsville Rd.
Rochester, NY 14624
(716) 235-6910

American Association of Spinal Cord Injury Psychologists
and Social Workers
75-20 Astoria Blvd.
Jackson Heights, NY 11370-1177
(718) 803-3782

American Association of Suicidology
2459 S. Ash
Denver, CO 80222
(303) 692-0985

American Board of Sexology
1929 18th St., Suite 1166
Washington, DC 20009
(202) 462-2122

American Chiropractic Association
1701 Clarendon Blvd.
Arlington, VA 22209
(703) 276-8800

American Chronic Pain Association—World Headquarters.
(Self-help groups for chronic pain sufferers. Contact them to find out about
your local groups.)
P.O. Box 850
Rocklin, CA 95677
(916) 632-0922

American College of Nutrition
722 Robert E. Lee Drive
Wilmington, NC 28412-0927
(919) 452-1222

American College of Preventive Medicine
1600 L St., NW, Suite 206
Washington, DC 20036
(202) 466-2044

American Congress of Rehabilitation Medicine
5700 Old Orchard Road, 1st Floor
Skokie, IL 60077-1057
(708) 966-0095

American Dance Therapy Association
2000 Century Plaza, Suite 108
Columbia, MD 21044
(410) 997-4040

American Dietetic Association
216 W. Jackson Blvd., Suite 800
Chicago, IL 60606-6995
(312) 899-0040

American Group Psychotherapy Association
25 East 21st St., 6th Floor
New York, NY 10010
(212) 477-2677

American Herbal Products Association
P.O. Box 2410
Austin, TX 78768
(512) 320-8555

American Holistic Medical Association
4101 Lake Boone Trail, Suite 201
Raleigh, NC 27607-6518
(919) 787-5146

American Holistic Nurses' Association
4101 Lake Boone Trail, Suite 201
Raleigh, NC 27607-6518
(919) 787-5181

American Institute of Homeopathy
1585 Glencoe St., Suite 44
Denver, CO 80220
(303) 898-5477

American Lung Association
1740 Broadway, 16th Floor
New York, NY 10019-4374
(212) 315-8700

American Massage Therapy Association
820 Davis St., Suite 100
Evanston, IL 60201-4444
(708) 864-0123

American Oriental Body Therapy Association
6801 Jericho Turnpike
Syossset, NY 11791-4416
(516) 364-5533

American Pain Society
5700 Old Orchard Road, 1st Floor
Skokie, IL 60077-1024
(708) 966-5595

American Physical Therapy Association
1111 N. Fairfax St.
Alexandria, VA 22314-1488
(703) 684-2782

American Polarity Therapy Association
4101 Lake Boone Trail, Suite 201
Raleigh, NC 27607-6518
(919) 787-5181

American Psychiatric Association
1400 K. St. N.W.
Washington, DC 20005
(202) 682-6000

American Psychological Association
750 First St. N.E.
Washington, DC 20002-4242
(202) 336-5500

American Rehabilitation Counseling Association
5999 Steveson Ave.
Alexandria, VA 22304-3300
(703) 823-9800

American Self-Help Clearinghouse (Database of self-help groups)
St. Clares Riverside Medical Center
Denville, NJ 07834
(201) 625-7101

American Society for Psychical Research
5 W. 73rd St.
New York, NY 10023
(212) 799-5050

American Therapeutic Recreation Association
P.O. Box 15215
Hattiesburg, MS 39404-5215
(800) 553-0304

American Trauma Society
8903 Presidential Pkwy., Suite 512
Upper Marlboro, MD 20772-2656
(301) 420-4189

Association for Advancement of Behavior Therapy
805 Seventh Avenue, Suite 16A
New York, NY 10001
(212) 647-1890

Association for Applied Psychophysiology and Biofeedback
10200 West 44th Ave., Suite 304
Wheat Ridge, CO 80033
(303) 422-8436

Association for Humanistic Psychology
1772 Vallejo, Suite 3
San Francisco, CA 94123-9816
(415) 346-7929

Association for the Care of Children's Health
7910 Woodmont Ave., Suite 300
Bethesda, MD 20814-3015
(301) 654-6549

Association to Advance Ethical Hypnosis
2675 Oakwood Drive
Cuyahoga Falls, OH 44221
(216) 923-8880

Association for Research and Enlightenment
215 67th St.
Virginia Beach, VA 23451
(804) 428-3588

Association for Transpersonal Psychology
P.O. Box 3049
Stanford, CA 94309
(415) 327-2066

Borderland Sciences Research Foundation
P.O. Box 220
Bayside, CA 95524
(707) 825-7733

Council for Exceptional Children
1920 Association Drive
Reston, VA 22091-1589
(703) 620-3660

Council for Learning Disabilities
P.O. Box 40303
Overland Park, KS 66204
(913) 492-8755

Council of Colleges of Acupuncture and Oriental Medicine
1424 16th St. N.W., Suite 501
Washington, DC 20036-2211
(202) 265-3370

Fellowship for Spiritual Understanding
P.O. Box 816
Palos Verdes Estates, CA 90274
(213) 373-2669

Foundation for Research on Nature of Man
402 N. Buchanan Blvd.
Durham, NC 27701
(919) 688-8241

Holistic Health Association
360 Nassau Street
Princeton, NJ 08540-4615
(609) 924-8580

Inner Peace Movement
P.O. Box 4900
Washington, DC 20008
(515) 342-4576

International Academy of Nutrition and Preventive Medicine
P.O. Box 18433
Asheville, NC 28814-0433
(704) 258-3243

International Association of Professional Natural Hygienists
204 Stambaugh Building
Youngstown, OH 44503-1635
(216) 746-5000

International Chiropractors Association
1110 N. Glebe Road, Suite 1000
Arlington, VA 22201
(703) 528-5000

International New Thought Alliance
5003 E. Broadway Road
Mesa, AZ 85206
(602) 830-2461

International Reading Association (Clearinghouse that promotes improved reading instruction and literacy.)
800 Barksdale Rd., P.O. Box 8139
Newark, DE 19714
(302) 731-1600

Learning Light Foundation
1212 E. Lincoln Avenue
Anaheim, CA 92805
(714) 533-2311

Mind Science Foundation
7979 Broadway, Suite 100
San Antonio, TX 78209
(210) 821-6094

The Ultimate Power

National Association for Music Therapy
8455 Colesville Rd., Suite 930
Silver Spring, MD 20910-3319
(301) 589-3300

National Association of Arts Therapies Associations
2000 Century Plaza, Suite 108
c/o American Dance Therapy Association
Columbia, MD 21044
(304) 379-3301

National Speakers Association—World Headquarters
(This is a self-help group for individuals currently involved in the business of professional speaking.)
1500 South Priest Drive
Tempe, Arizona 85281
Tel (602) 968-2552 Fax (602) 968-0911

Serendipity Association for Research and Implementation
7010 Casa Lane, #5
Lemon Grove, CA 91945

Society of Behavioral Medicine
103 South Adams St.
Rockville, MD 20850
(301) 251-2790

Spiritual Advisory Council
P.O. Box 7868
Philadelphia, PA 19101

Spiritual Wellness Network
523 N. 66th Street
Wauwatosa, WI 53213
(414) 453-8751

The Arlin J. Brown Information Center
P.O. Box 251
Ft. Belvoir, VA 22060
(703) 752-9511

Toastmasters International—World Headquarters.
(This is a self-help group for those who want to build self-esteem and learn how to speak in public. First look in your phone book under Toastmasters International.)
P.O. Box 9052
Mission Viejo, CA 92690
(714) 858-8255

United States Psychotronics Association
P.O. Box 354
Wilmette, IL 60091
(708) 733-0116

Canada

Action League of Physically Handicapped Adults
1940 Oxford Street East, Suite 8
London, Ontario N5V 2Z8
(519) 433-7221

Active Living Alliance for Canadians with a Disability
1600 James Naismith Dr., Suite 312
Gloucester, Ontario K1B 5N4
(613) 478-5747

Advocacy Group for the Environmentally Sensitive
1887 Chaine Ct.
Orleans, Ontario K1C 2W6
(613) 830-5722

Alcoholics Anonymous World Service Inc. (First look in local phone book under Al-Anon.)
P.O. Box 459, Grand Central Station
New York, NY 10163 USA
(212) 870-3400

Allergy Foundation of Canada
P.O. Box 1904
Saskatoon, Saskatchewan S7K 3S5
(306) 373-7591

Alliance for a Drug-Free Canada
P.O. Box 355, Station A
Toronto, Ontario M5W 1C5
(416) 730-4217

The Ultimate Power

American Chronic Pain Association—World Headquarters
(Self-help groups for chronic pain sufferers. Contact them to find your local group.)
P.O. Box 850
Rocklin, CA 95677 USA
(916) 632-0922

Association of Naturopathic Physicians
2786 West 16 St., Suite 204
Vancouver, British Columbia V6K 3C4
(604) 732-7070

Association for Social Psychology
P.O. Box 152, Stn. O
Toronto, Ontario M4A 2N3

Health Action Network Society
5262 Rumble St.
Burnaby, British Columbia V5J 2B6
(604) 435-0512

Humanist Association of Canada (Coalition for secular humanism and free thought.)
P.O. Box 3736, Stn C
Ottawa, Ontario K1Y 4J8
(613) 722-4652

Inner Peace Movement of Canada (Promotes self-help groups and techniques.)
100 Bronson Ave., Suite 1106
Ottawa, Ontario K1R 6G8
(613) 238-7844

Institute of Positive Health for Seniors Inc.
43 Bruyere St.
Ottawa, Ontario KIN 5C8

International Federation of Physical Medicine & Rehabilitation
Mount Sinai Hospital, Dept. Rehab. Medicine, 600 University Ave.
Toronto, Ontario M5G 1X5
(416) 586-5033

International Nutritional Immunology Group
Janeway Child Health Centre
St. John's, Newfoundland A1A 1R8
(709) 778-4519

International Society for Neuropathology
Dept. of Pathology, Richardson Laboratory, Queens University
Kingston, Ontario K7L 3N6
(613) 545-2818

Kids Help Foundation (Maintains data base of 23,000 emergency services for children.)
60 Bloor Street West, Suite 1101
Toronto, Ontario M4W 1A1
(416) 920-5437

Learning Disabilities Association of Canada
323 Chapel St., Suite 200
Ottawa, Ontario K1N 7Z2
(613) 238-5721

Massage Therapists Association of Nova Scotia
7193 Quinppol Rd.
Halifax, Nova Scotia B3L 1C7
(902) 453-5588

Massage Therapy Association of British Columbia
5620 Bessborough Dr.
Burnaby, British Columbia V5B 1E2
(604) 946-1168

Massage Therapy Association of Manitoba
P.O. Box 63063
Winnipeg, Manitoba R3L 2V8

National Chiropractors Society of Canada
180 Elgin St.
Ottawa, Ontario K2P 2K7

National Eating Disorders Centre
Women's College Hospital
College Wing 1-304
200 Elizabeth Street
Toronto, Ontario M5G 2C4
(416) 340-4156

National Educational Association of Disabled Students
Carleton University, 4th Level Unicentre
1125 Colonel By Dr.
Ottawa, Ontario K1S 5B6
(613) 233-5963

National Speakers Association—World Headquarters
(This is a self-help group for individuals currently involved
in the business of professional speaking.)
1500 South Priest Drive
Tempe, AZ 85281 USA
(602) 968-2552 Fax (602) 968-0911

Ontario Massage Therapists Association
950 Yonge St., Suite 1007
Toronto, Ontario M4W 2J4
(416) 968-6487

Physicians for a Smoke-Free Canada
P.O. Box 4849, Stn. E
Ottawa, Ontario K1S 5J1
(613) 233-4878

Self-Help Clearinghouse (Database of self-help groups.)
40 Orchard View Blvd.
Suite 219—Library Building
Toronto, Ontario M4R 1B9
(416) 487-4355

Toastmasters International—World Headquarters
(This is a self-help group for those who want to build
self-esteem and learn how to speak in public. First look
in your phone book under Toastmasters International.)
P.O. Box 9052
Mission Viejo, CA 92690
(714) 858-8255

Australia

Alcoholics Anonymous World Service Inc.
(First look in local phone book under Al-Anon.)
P.O. Box 459, Grand Central Station
New York, NY 10163 USA
(212) 870-3400

American Chronic Pain Association—World Headquarters
(Self-help groups for chronic pain sufferers. Contact them
to find out about your local group.)
P.O. Box 850
Rocklin, CA 95677 USA
(916) 632-0922

Association of Massage Therapists (N.S.W.)
3/33 Denham St.
Bondi
NSW 2026
(02) 300-9405

Australasian Society for Immunology Inc.
C/- VMPF, 293 Royal Pde
Parkville
Vic. 3052
(03) 347-9633

Australian Council for Health, Physical Education and Recreation
214 Port Rd.
Hindmarsh
SA 5007
(08) 340-3388

Australian Health Professionals Association
5th Fl., 54 Victoria St.
Carlton
Vic. 3053
(03) 663-3011

Australian Institute of Environmental Health
8 Geils Crt
Deakin
Act 2600
(06) 285-3119

Australian Federation of Homeopaths NSW Branch
7/29 Bertram St.
Chatswood
NSW 2067
(02) 415-3928

Australian Hypnotherapy Association
20 Larool Crescent
Castle Hill
NSW 2154
(02) 634-4915

Australian Institute of Homeopathy
7/29 Bertram St
Chatswood
NSW 2067
(02) 415-3928

Australian Natural Therapists Association
P.O. Box 308
Melrose Park
SA 5039
(08) 371-3222

Australian Society of Hypnosis, The
1st Fl. Austin Hospital
Heidelberg
Vic. 3084
(03) 459-6499

Collective of Self-Help and Health (Database of self-help groups.)
247-251 Flinders Lane
Melbourne 3000
(03) 650-1455/1488

Consumers' Health Forum of Australia
Old Lyons Prim. School, 67
Launceston St. Lyons
ACT 2606
(06) 281-0811

Dr. Edward Bach Society of Australia
Narwee Pre School
Bryant St, Narwee
NSW 2209
(02) 570-2731

Institute for Fitness Research and Training
64 MacKinnon Pde.
North Adelaide
SA 5006
(08) 267-1887

Keep Fit SA
84 Archer St
North Adelaide
SA 5006
(08) 239-2077

National Health and Medical Research Council
Albemarle Building
Furzer St, Woden
ACT 2606
(06) 289-7019

National Herbalists Association of Australia
14/247-49 Kingsgrove Rd.
Kingsgrove
NSW 2208
(02) 502-2938

Natural Health Society of Australia
Suite 28, 541 High St.
Penrith
NSW 2750
(047) 21-5068

National Speakers Association—World Headquarters
(This is a self-help group for individuals currently
involved in the business of professional speaking.)
1500 South Priest Drive
Tempe, AZ 85281 USA
Tel (602) 968-2552 Fax (602) 968-0911

NSW Association of Health Professions
82 Christie St.
St Leonards
NSW 2065
(02) 438-1833

Nutritional Foods Association
Ste 79, Chatswood Village
Oscar St. Chatswood
NSW 2067
(02) 441-6348

Pritikin Health Association of Australia
59 Upolo Esplanade
Clifton Beach
Qld 4879
(070) 59-1610

Prostitutes Association of the NT for Health Education and Referral
Office 1, 64 Smith St.
Darwin
NT 0800
(089) 41-0633

Public Health Association of Australia
9 Napier Cl
Deakin
ACT 2601
(06) 285-2373

Queensland Association for Quality Assurance in Health Care
PO Box 412
Moorooka
Qld. 4105
(07) 275-6359

Royal Queensland Bush Children's Health Scheme
Lvl 5, BP Hse, 193 Nth Quay
Brisbane
Qld. 4000
(07) 236-2155

Society of Clinical Masseurs Inc., The
9 Delhi
Mitcham
Vic 3132
(03) 874-6973

South Australian Association of Hypnotherapists Inc.
78 Goodwood
Wayville
SA 5034
(08) 373-3381

Student Initiative in Community Health
c/- SRC Wentworth Bldg
Uni of Sydney
NSW 2006
(02) 660-5222

Toastmasters International—World Headquarters
(This is a self-help group for those who want to build self-esteem and learn how to speak in public. First look in your phone book under Toastmasters International.)
P.O. Box 9052
Mission Viejo, CA 92690 USA
(714) 858-8255

Vegetarian Society of South Australia Inc.
Box 46
Rundle Mall
SA 5000
(08) 261-3194

Women's Health Care Association Inc.
100 Aberdeen St
Northbridge
WA 6003
(09) 227-8122

United Kingdom

American Chronic Pain Association—World Headquarters
(Self-help groups for chronic pain sufferers. Contact them
to find out about your local group.)
P.O. Box 850
Rocklin, CA 95677 USA
(916) 632-0922

Association for Prevention of Addiction
37-39 Great Guildford St.
London SE1 0ES
(071) 620-1919

Barnado's (Assists children, youths and families with disadvantages or
disabilities.)
Tanners Lane, Barkingside
Ilford, Essex IG6 1QG
(081) 550-8822

British Acupuncture Association and Register
34 Alderney St.
London SW1V 4EU
(071) 834-1012

British Herbal Medicine Association
Field House, Lye Hole Lane, Redhill
Bristol, Avon BS18 7TB
(0934) 862994

British Holistic Medical Association
179 Gloucester Place
London, NW1 6DX
(071) 262-5299

British Homeopathic Association
27a Devonshire St.
London, W1N 1RJ
(071) 935-2163

British Hypnotherapy Association
67 Upper Berkeley St.
London W1H 7DH
(071) 723-4443

The Ultimate Power

British Medical Acupuncture Society
Newton House, Newton Lane, Whitley
Warrington, Chesire WA4 4JA
(0925) 730727

British Psychological Society
St. Andrews House, 48 Princess Rd. East
Liecester, Leicestershire LE1 7DR
(0533) 549568

British Society for Music Therapy
25 Rosslyn Avenue, Barnet
Hertfordshire EN4 8DH
(081) 368 8879

Children's Society, The
Edward Rudolf House, Margery St.
London WC1X 0JL
(071) 837 4299

Coronary Prevention Group
Plantation House, 31-35 Fenchurch Street
London EC3M 3NN
(071) 837 4299

Council for Complementary and Alternative Medicine
179 Gloucester Place
London NW1 6DX
(071) 724 9103

Disability Action
2 Annadale Avenue, Belfast
Co Antrim BT7 3UR
(0232) 491011

Disability Scotland
Princes House, 5 Shandwick Place
Edinburgh, Midlothian EH2 4RG
(031) 229 8632

Disabled Living
Redbank House, 4 Chad's St., Cheetham
Manchester, Lancashire M8 8QA
(061) 832 3678

Disabled Living Foundation
380-384 Harrow Rd.
London W9 2HU
(071) 289 6111

Disfigurement Guidance Centre/Laserfair
P.O. Box 7, Cupar
Fife KY15 4PF
(0334) 839084

Eating Disorders Association
Sackville Place, 44 Magdalen St.
Norwich, Norfolk NR3 1JU
(0603) 621414

Empathy Ltd. (Promotes employment opportunities for people with disabilities.)
c/o Hereward College, Bramston Crescent, Tile Hill Lane
Coventry, West Midlands CV4 9SW
(0203) 422042

Enable (Promotes welfare of learning disabled people.)
13 Elmbank St., Glasgow
Lanarkshire G2 4QA
(041) 226 4541

General Council and Register of Naturopaths
Frazer House, 6 Netherhall Gardens
London NW3 5RR
(071) 435 8728

Health Food Manufacturers' Association
Angel Court, High St.
Godalming, Surrey GU7 1DT
(0483) 426450

Hyperactive Children's Support Group
71 Whyke Lane, Chichester
West Sussex PO19 2LD
(0903) 725182

Institute of Chiropodists
91 Lord St., Southport
Merseyside PR8 1SA
(0704) 546141

Institute for Optimum Nutrition (Public education on the benefits of optimum nutrition.)
5 Jerdan Place
London SW6 1BE
(071) 385 7984

International Federation of Essential Oils & Aroma Trades
Suite 309-315, Kemp House
152/160 City Rd., London EC1V 2NP
(071) 253 9421

MIND (National Association for Mental Health)
22 Harley St.
London W1N 2ED
(071) 637 0741

Manic Depression Fellowship
13 Rosslyn Rd., Twickenham
Middlesex TW1 2AR
(081) 892 2811

National Association of Health Stores
Unit D2, Boston Industrial Centre, Norfolk St.
Boston, Lincoinshire PE21 9HG
(0205) 362626

National Institute of Medical Herbalists
9 Palace Gate, Exeter
Devon EX1 1JA
(0392) 426022

National Self-Help Support Centre, NCVO
26 Bedford Square, London, WC1B 3HU
(071) 636-4066

National Speakers Association—World Headquarters
(This is a self-help group for individuals currently involved in the business of professional speaking.)
1500 South Priest Drive
Tempe, AZ 85281 USA
Tel (602) 968-2552 Fax (602) 968-0911

Natural Medicines Society
Edith Lewis House, Ilkeston
Derbyshire DE7 8EJ
(0602) 329454

New Approaches to Cancer
Colin Ryder Richardson, 5 Larksfield
Egham, Surrey TW2O ORB
(0784) 433610

Patients' Association (Promotes access to self help groups and handles complaints.)
18 Victoria Park Square, Bethnal Green
London E2 9PF
(081) 981 5676

Psionic Medical Association (Homeopathic medicine society.)
Garden College, Beacon Hill Park
Hindhead, Surrey GU26 6HU
(0428) 605752

Royal Association for Disability and Rehabilitation
28 Portland Place
London W1N 4DE
(071) 580 9194

School of Phytotherapy/Herbal Medicine
Bucksteep Manor, Bodle St. Green
Halisham, East Sussex BN27 4RJ
(0323) 833812

Self-Help Centre, NCVO
Regent's Wharf, 8 All Saints St.
London N1 9RL
(071) 713 6161

Self-Help Team (Database of self-help groups.)
20 Pelham Road, Sherwood Rise
Nottingham, NG5 1AP
(0602) 691212

Society of Homeopaths
2 Artizan Rd., Northampton
Northamptonshire NN1 4HU
(0604) 21400

Toastmasters International—World Headquarters
(This is a self-help group for those who want to build
self-esteem and learn how to speak in public. First look
in your phone book under Toastmasters International.)
P.O. Box 9052
Mission Viejo, CA 92690 USA
(714) 858-8255

The Ultimate Power

Traditional Acupuncture Society
1 The Ridgeway, Stratford upon Avon
Warwickshire CV37 9JL
(0789) 298798

Turning Point (Learning disabilities, drug, alcohol and mental health resources.)
New Loom House, 101 Backchurch Lane
London E1 1LU
(071) 702 2300

Bibliography
and Suggested Readings

Aromatherapy

Lee, William H. and Lynn, *The Book of Practical Aromatherapy*, New Canaan: Keats Publishing, Inc. (1992)

Worwood, Valerie Ann, *The Complete Book of Essential Oils & Aromatherapy*, San Rafael: New World Library (1991)

Healing (See also Psychology / Self-Help / Spirituality and Spiritual Healing)

Anderson, Deborah and Martha Finne, *Michael's Story: Emotional Abuse and Working With a Counselor*, Minneapolis: Dillon Press (1986)

Benson, Herbert, *The Relaxation Response*, New York: William Morrow (1975)

_____, *Beyond The Relaxation Response*, New York: Times Books (1984)

Benson, Herbert and Eileen M. Stuart, *The Wellness Book: The Comprehensive Guide to Maintaining and Treating Stress Related Illness*, New York: Fireside (1992)

Cassini, Kathleen and Jaqueline Rogers, *I Want to Help But I Don't Know How*, Cincinnati: Griefwork, Inc. (1985)

Cypert, Samuel, Believe and Achieve: *W. Clement Stone's 17 Principles of Success*, New York: Avon Books (1991)

Dillon, Ilene, *Bouncing Back After Anger and Argument*, Fairfax: Rise Publications (1985)

Dossey, Larry, *Meaning & Medicine*, New York: Bantam Books (1991)

Gil, Eliana, *Outgrowing the Pain: A Book for and About Adults Abused as Children*, San Francisco: Launch Press (1983)

Kushner, Harold, *When Bad Things Happen to Good People*, New York: Avon (1981)

Lerner, Harriet, *The Dance of Anger*, New York: Harper & Row (1989)

———, *The Dance of Deception*, New York: HarperCollins Publishers (1993)

Melzack, Ronald and Patrick Wall, *The Challenge of Pain*, Markham: Penguin Books (1982)

Quezada, Adolfo, *Goodbye, My Son, Hello*, St. Meriand: Abbey Press (1985)

Rossman, M. *Healing Yourself*, New York: Pocket Books (1990)

Travis, Carol, *Anger: The Misunderstood Emotion*, New York: Simon & Shuster (1984)

Veninga, Robert, *A Gift of Hope: How We Survive Our Tragedies*, New York: Ballantine Books (1985)

Health (See also Nutrition)

Balch, James F. and Phyllis A., *Prescription for Nutritional Healing: A Practical A-Z Reference to Drug-free Remedies Using Vitamins,*

Minerals, Herbs & Food Supplements Garden City Park: Avery Publishing Group Inc. (1990)

Chopra, Deepak, *Ageless Body, Timeless Mind: The Quantum Alternative to Growing Old*, New York: Harmony Books (1993)

Diamond, Harvey and Marilyn, *Fit for Life II: Living Health, The Complete Health Program*, New York: Warner Books (1988)

Dunne, Lavon, *Nutrition Almanac*, Toronto: McGraw-Hill (1990)

Feltman, John, *The Prevention How-To Dictionary of Healing Remedies and Techniques*, Emmaus: Rodale Press (1992)

Great Saint Ormand Street Hospital Study: Hyperactivity and the Role of Food in Children, London: Great Saint Ormand Street Hospital (refer to *Little Monsters*, Television video.)

Little Monsters, Television video show, London: British Broadcasting Corporation (1992)

Mabey, Richard, *The New Age Herbalist*, New York: Macmillan Publishing Company (1988)

Mindell, Earl, *Vitamin Bible*, New York: Warner Books (1991)

Moyers, Bill, *Healing and the Mind*, New York: Bantam Doubleday Dell Audio Publishing (1993)

Ornish, Dr. Dean, *Dr. Dean Ornish's Program for Reversing Heart Disease*, New York: Random House (1990)

Robbins, John, *Diet for a New America*, Walpole: Stillpoint Publishing (1987)

_____, *May All Be Fed: Diet for a New World*, New York: Avon Books (1993)

Salaman, Maureen and James Scheer, *Foods that Heal*, Menlo Park: Statford Publishing (1989)

Siegel, Dr. Bernie, *Love, Medicine and Miracles*, New York: Harper & Row (1986)

_____, *Peace, Love and Healing*, New York: Harper & Row (1989)

Tracy, Lisa, *The Gradual Vegetarian*, New York: Dell Publishing (1993)

Meditation

Hanh, T.N., *The Miracle of Mindfulness: A Manual on Meditation*, Boston: Beacon Press (1976)

LeShan, L., *How to Meditate*, New York: Bantam, (1974)

New Thought (See Healing / Health / Philosophy / Psychology / Self-Help / Spiritual / Spiritual Healing)

Nutrition (See Health / Philosophy See also Self-Help / Spirituality / Spiritual Healing)

Chai, Ch'u and Winberg Chai, *Confucianism*, Hauppauge: Barron's Educational Series, Inc. (1973)

Winokur, Jon, *Zen To Go*, New York: New American Library (1989)

Psychology (See Healing / Self-Help / Spirituality and Spiritual Healing)

Self-Help (See also Healing / Psychology / Spirituality and Spiritual Healing)

Branden, Nathaniel, *To See What I See and Know What I Know*, New York: Bantam (1986)

Burns, D.D., *The Feeling Good Handbook: Using the New Mood Therapy in Everyday Life*, New York: William Morrow (1989)

Carnegie, Dale, *How To Win Friends and Influence People*, New York: Pocket Books (1992)

Cousins, Norman, *Anatomy of an Illness*, New York: W. W. Norton (1979)

Covey, Stephen, *The 7 Habits of Highly Effective People*, New York: Fireside (1990)

Dyer, Dr. Wayne, *Your Erroneous Zones*, New York: Harper Paperbacks (1993)

_____, Real Magic, New York: Harper Paperbacks (1994)

Fulghum, Robert, *All I Really Need To Know I Learned In Kindergarten*, New York: Ivy Books (1991)

Gawain, Shakti, *Creative Visualization*, New York: Bantam Books (1982)

Harris, Dr. Thomas, *I'm OK—You're OK*, New York: Avon Books (1973)

Jung, Carl, *Man and His Symbols*, New York: Dell Publishing (1968)

Laing, R.D., *The Politics of the Family*, Toronto: CBC Enterprises (1983)

Lerner, Harriet G., *The Dance of Deception*, New York: HarperCollins (1993)

Locke, S. and D. Colligan, *The Healer Within*, New York: Mentor Books (1987)

Mandino, Og, *The Greatest Success in the World*, New York: Bantam (1982)

_____, *The Greatest Salesman in the World*, New York: Bantam (1983)

_____, *The Greatest Miracle in the World*, New York: Bantam (1988)

_____, *A Better Way To Live*, New York: Bantam (1990)

O'Conner, Joseph and John Seymour, *Introducing NLP: Neuro-Linguistic Programming: Psychological Skills for Understanding and Influencing People*, San Francisco: The Aquarian Press (1993)

Robbins, Anthony, *Awaken the Giant Within*, New York: Simon & Shuster (1992)

The Prevention Pain-Relief System: A Total Program for Relieving Any Pain in Your Body, edited by Alice Feinstein, Emmaus: Rodale Press (1992)

Twerski, Abraham, *Self-Discovery in Recovery*, Toronto: Harper & Row (1989)

Spirituality and Spiritual Healing (See also Philosophy)

Alcoholics Anonymous World Services, Inc. Staff, *Alcoholics Anonymous, The Story of How Many Thousands of Men and Women Have Recovered from Alcoholism*, New York (1990)

Bach, Richard, *Jonathan Livingston Seagull*, New York: Avon Books (1970)
_____, *Illusions—The Adventures of a Reluctant Messiah*, New York: Dell Publishing (1989)

Frankl, V., *Man's Search for Meaning*, Boston: Beacon Press (1963)

Gibran, Kahlil, *The Prophet*, Toronto: Penguin Books (1992)

Gilhuis, Cornelis, *Conversations on Growing Older*, Grand Rapids: William B. Eerdmans Publishing Company (1977)

Greenwood, Dr. Michael and Dr. Peter Nunn, *Paradox & Healing*, Victoria: Paradox Publishers (1994)

Kushner, Harold, *When Bad Things Happen to Good People*, New York: Summit Books (1982)

_____, *When All You've Ever Wanted Isn't Enough*, New York: Summit Books (1986)

Redfield, James, *The Celestine Prophecy: An Adventure*, New York: Warner Books (1994)

Vaughan, Frances and Roger Walsh, *Accept This Gift: Selections from a Course in Miracles*, New York: J. P. Tarcher (1992)

Index

V

W

Y

Do you want to find out more about alternative health options?

Write for information about Ken's newsletter dedicated to seeking alternatives. You will discover ancient folklore and modern options as Ken seeks and uncovers them for you. From acupressure to zone therapy, a universe of choices will open for your benefit. Write: The Love Living & Live Loving Series™ Newsletter, c/o Adi, Gaia, Esalen Publications Inc., 8391 Beverly Blvd, Suite 323-UP, Los Angeles, CA 90048.

A Great Gift for the Special People In Your Life!

ORDER FORM

YES, I want to order this compelling book. Send me _____ copies of *The Ultimate Power* at $14.95 plus $3.50 each for shipping and handling. New York residents add $1.05 sales tax. Please allow four weeks for delivery.

Name _____

Phone _____

Organization _____

Address _____

City/State/Zip _____

My check or money order for $ _____ is enclosed.

Charge my   ☐ VISA   ☐ MasterCard   ☐ AMEX

Card number _____ Exp _____

Signature _____

Please make your check or money order payable and return to:

AGES Publications
8391 Beverly Blvd., Ste. 323-AB
Los Angeles, CA 90048

Call your credit card orders toll-free to:
1-800-263-1991